Regulating Death

Regulating Death

Euthanasia and the Case of the Netherlands

CARLOS F. GOMEZ, M.D.

Foreword by Leon R. Kass, M.D.

THE FREE PRESS
A Division of Macmillan, Inc.
NEW YORK
Maxwell Macmillan Canada
TORONTO
Maxwell Macmillan International
NEW YORK   OXFORD   SINGAPORE   SYDNEY

The Free Press
A Division of Macmillan, Inc.
866 Third Avenue, New York, N.Y. 10022

Maxwell Macmillan Canada, Inc.
1200 Eglinton Avenue East
Suite 200
Don Mills, Ontario M3C 3N1

Macmillan, Inc. is part of the Maxwell Communication Group of Companies.

Printed in the United States of America

printing number
1 2 3 4 5 6 7 8 9 10

Library of Congress Cataloging-in-Publication Data

Gomez, Carlos F.
    Regulating death: euthanasia and the case of the Netherlands/
Carlos F. Gomez; foreword by Leon R. Kass.
        p.   cm.
    Includes bibliographical references and index.
    ISBN 0-02-912440-9
    1. Euthanasia—Netherlands.   I. Title.
R726.G58   1991
179' .7—dc20   91–14459
                                                        CIP

To Madeleine

Contents

—— *Foreword* ——

Leon R. Kass, M.D.

Regulating Death. The very notion smacks of pride if not absurdity; for how can human beings rule over fate and fatality, by definition unregulatable? Preposterous or not, the fight to master necessity, disease, and death has been the major campaign of the modern scientific project, waged—especially in this half century—with increasing success. But the success is not yet complete, and, indeed, increasingly it feels like failure. For we who, thanks to medicine, are living longer are living long enough to finish life in protracted periods of debility, dementia, dependence, and disgrace—with medicine impotent to do more than treat the supervening acute infections that, left untreated, would allow us a merciful exit. What are we to do? Many still look to science in hope of further triumphs in the war against mortality and decay. Others, in despair here and now, want to exercise greater control over the end of life by electing death to avoid the burdens of lingering on. The failures resulting from attempts to rule over death are to be resolved by placing death still further under our own control.

Euthanasia is an idea whose time seems to be coming to America. With many of us suffering, and more of us fearing, a horrible and degraded end of life, efforts to legalize mercy killing—or voluntary euthanasia or physician-assisted suicide—gain support across the country. Many physicians are apparently willing to participate. There remains, to be sure, strong opposition, usually on religious grounds, to such willful taking of an innocent life, even on request. Others fear for the corruption of, or the loss of trust in, the medical profession should physicians become dispensers of death. Everyone—even those in favor of euthanasia—recognize the possible abuses, among them the coercion of consent and the slide into killing the weak and the unwanted without their consent. To allay these fears, partisans of euthanasia point to the Netherlands, where for over a decade physicians have been practicing mercy killing with the acquiescence if not the wholehearted support of the law and the larger society. If Holland, without doubt a highly civilized, liberal, and humane nation—indeed, in World War II a bastion of principled decency against the unspeakable assaults on human life—opts for mercy killing and practices it without abuse, we can take heart and proceed gently into that good night. Let us look to the Dutch.

This is just what Carlos Gomez has done. Not content with pious pronouncements and reassurances, he went to the Netherlands to see for himself. He interviewed jurists about the law and physicians about their practice. He was especially eager to discover how the Dutch *in fact* control euthanasia, how they keep it from being practiced on those who do not request it, and how they provide for public accountability. His interests were in many quarters viewed with suspicion, and many physicians refused to speak with him. Yet what he learned from the cooperative ones—who, it seems fair to assume, felt they had least to hide—is anything but reassuring. For he found that the Dutch physicians fail to observe their own *self-imposed* guidelines and standards, intended to regulate the practice of euthanasia: they sometimes do not seek a second opinion before electing death; they usually do not report the deed or even note it on the death certificate; where they do report euthanasia, no one investigates the facts; where someone does investigate, the physician controls all the evidence; and they euthanize some patients who have not clearly requested death. Although the Dutch believe they have a well-regulated practice, Gomez shows instead that they have an *unregulated* practice. And he makes us wonder whether regulating euthanasia is even possible: for how can one insist that euthanasia is and ought to be a matter for private choice, best handled privately between patient and doctor, and yet expect there to be appropriate oversight, public accountability, and control? Must we, can we, should we rely solely on the virtue of the medical profession—and each of its unregulated practitioners—to protect the exposed and vulnerable lives of the infirm, the elderly, and the powerless, who, incapable of real autonomy, will be deemed by others to have lives no longer worth living or, more likely, no longer worth sustaining at great medical expense?

We will, I fear, continue to believe in our own technique. When medicine fails our unreasonable expectations, we will prefer the technical solution of a medically administered death, trusting to our techniques of regulation—including guidelines, protocols, and hospital ethics committees—to keep everything under control. Never mind the old taboos against suicide and killing and never mind the Hippocratic Oath: reason alone can guide us; death can be regulated. This perilous confidence is supported only by our naïveté. Thanks to Carlos Gomez and his sobering research, we need not remain naïve. The friends of human life and human decency are hereby properly forewarned.

—— *Preface* ——

This study is born, in part, out of a sense of uneasiness and dissatisfaction with the current debate in the United States on the permissibility of euthanasia. What was once a small, if insistent, band of voices that advocated euthanasia under some circumstances has grown in both number and volume. It is a band of voices that has newly found legitimacy and has captured the attention of a serious audience in professional medical circles. This reawakened interest in euthanasia has also generated political activity, with organized legislative movements in at least three states (Washington, Oregon, and California) seeking to overturn existing laws that prohibit physicians from intentionally killing patients.

The public focus of concern in this debate has been those patients afflicted with a terminal disease who are dying a slow, disfiguring death. Exhausted from their struggle, dispirited over their prospects, and facing weeks or months of pain, these patients, it is argued, should be offered something that does no more than hasten the inevitable. If they are competent to make decisions—and if they are so inclined—these patients should be allowed to seek assistance with suicide. More specifically, physicians should be permitted to administer a lethal drug at the patient's request.

Those who make this argument in favor of euthanasia—especially those now engaged in crafting new legislation—proceed from two premises, neither of which is easily refuted. The first is that to end a patient's suffering through euthanasia is a humane and charitable enterprise, that it fits well (or should fit well) with the traditionally accepted role of physician as alleviator of pain. When all else fails—when medicine's curatives and analgesics neither heal nor palliate—the physician should be able to end a consenting patient's suffering by killing the patient. The second premise, which complements the first, exalts the widely accepted principle of autonomy and suggests that freely consenting individuals—physicians and patients—should be relatively unfettered in this matter. If a patient so chooses to end his or her life and if a physician is a willing participant, then euthanasia is permissible. Laws, taboos, and professional canons of conduct that impinge on this freedom, that prohibit what is seen as a charitable act, should be modified or repealed. Moreover, so the argument goes, well-crafted legislation in this area has the added advantage of regulating a practice that occurs with greater frequency and regularity than we care to admit.

I am skeptical of these arguments (even in their most elegant form), and in particular, I am opposed to the end that they serve. There is a suasive power in these images of patients disfigured physically and emotionally by pain and illness, yet I am unconvinced that the proper response—either from the profession of medicine or from society as a whole—should be to assist in suicide. My objections have several sources. Some derive from a basic disagreement over what constitutes the fitting role of physicians in society and what part physicians may and may not play in their patients' lives. Other objections follow from a profound mistrust that what is portrayed as a charitable act is, in fact, beneficent and good: to acquiesce to a demand, however honest and sincere, is not necessarily the same as to act lovingly.

Were I to develop these objections more fully, this would be a rather different sort of study, focusing on matters more philosophical and theological. I leave that important task to others and instead concentrate here on a more specific worry: what will this newly codified practice of euthanasia look like? Will it be, as its defenders insist, an exercise of last resort, used only under the most rigidly controlled and tightly circumscribed of circumstances? What kinds of patients will ask for euthanasia, and how will we evaluate their requests? How will medicine assume this new role? That is, how will the profession respond to what is essentially a new task? Finally, and most importantly for the purposes of this study, how will the practice be controlled? How will we assure ourselves that the weak, the demented, the vulnerable, the stigmatized—those incapable of consent or dissent—not become the unwilling subjects of such a practice?

It is this latter concern that makes me the most uneasy, and even if I were won over by other arguments, prudence would still bid me to object to giving public sanction to the practice. The vulnerable among us are already more exposed than the rest to injustice in various forms;

some forms of injustice are more onerous and dangerous than others. No injustice, I would contend, would be greater than being put to death innocent of crime and unable to articulate one's interests. It is the possibility of this injustice that most hardens my resistance to calls for euthanasia.

Those who propose decriminalizing euthanasia under specific circumstances argue strongly that it is a practice that can, and should, be well controlled. Those who argue as I do, it is said, are denying dying patients a needed and welcome option because of misplaced and unfounded fears. There are certainly dangers here, the argument continues, but a mature and democratic society should be willing and able to construct a policy that enhances the autonomy of these dying patients while protecting the rights of others.

Of late, it has been at this point in the argument that proponents of euthanasia have pointed to the Netherlands as a model for this sort of practice. Some segments of the Dutch medical profession have practiced euthanasia, more or less openly, for more than a decade. Proponents of euthanasia in the United States look to Holland as evidence that this practice can be well managed and that it can be restricted only to those patients who are competent to make such a decision. The experience of the Dutch—who form a humane, tolerant, democratic society—should give some assurance that this practice does not *necessarily* degenerate into indiscriminate killing.

It is on precisely this subject—the regulatory mechanisms that govern euthanasia in the Netherlands—that there is a scarcity of information, especially in English-language documents and journals. There are, for instance, no reliable studies that evaluate the efficacy of those regulatory controls. Even the basic investigations, which would describe the practice of euthanasia, are scant. To suggest, then, that the experience of the Dutch on this matter is conclusive is to close prematurely an inquiry that has barely begun.

The aim of this study, then, is to describe and assess the practice of euthanasia in the Netherlands. More specifically, my goal is to elaborate on aspects of euthanasia that have yet to find their way into public debate and to discuss how the Dutch courts, legislature, and professional medical organizations have responded to the need to control a practice that even its most ardent supporters concede carries many dangers. In this study, I focus primarily on the policy aspects of the practice, that is, on the limiting role that both public and private institutions play in regulating euthanasia in the Netherlands. I evaluate the efficacy of those regulatory controls and suggest problems not only with the implementation of this practice but also with the broader theory used to justify the inclusion of euthanasia within medical practice.

My approach in this inquiry is to start with basic questions; that is, how do the Dutch understand the term *euthanasia* and what do they formally mean by this phrase? In Chapter 1, I rehearse the arguments of both opponents and proponents of the practice. My intent is not to construct a new defense or critique of euthanasia, *per se,* for that is a well-traveled road. Rather, I try to recast these arguments in terms more amenable to critical analysis.

Thus, for example, I begin by discussing the recent evolution of public control over medical practice—especially as it affects the intervention of medicine in our dying—as a way of elaborating on what I see as an irreducible tension between public goods and the private claims some of us make on those goods. I further suggest that death in a medical context has both private and public aspects, so there is already *some* limit to what any individual can claim as a right to assistance with their particular death. By way of example, I discuss my experiences with a group that helped to draft a public document on another contentious issue in medical practice (termination of treatment protocols), and suggest that one limit that society might reasonably impose derives from our abilities or inabilities to regulate a dangerous practice, particularly when the practice is reserved for a profession such as medicine, which serves people in particularly vulnerable circumstances.

Whether or not active euthanasia falls within publicly permissible limits of assistance with dying is a question I pursue by describing and analyzing the Dutch experience with euthanasia. At the end of the chapter, I draw parallels between the arguments of those in both countries who accept or defend euthanasia under certain circumstances, and I suggest ways in which the Dutch experience might, by analogy, be instructive to the American debate.

In Chapter 2, I describe the legal, political, and social context of euthanasia in the Netherlands. More specifically, I trace the development of the legal cases in that country that have created an opening for the practice of euthanasia, explain political problems that have kept euthanasia from being formally legalized, and elaborate on the checks that the Dutch have placed on the practice. I also document—to the extent that data are available—the prevalence of the practice. At the end of the chapter, I suggest that an uneasy consensus on the practice of euthanasia has evolved among the courts, the government, and the medical profession, and I point to some potential dangers in permitting the practice, especially in so unsettled an atmosphere.

The next two chapters focus on individual cases of euthanasia in the Netherlands (gathered during a recent trip) as a way of analyzing and testing the limits of the practice and by way of exploring the private side of euthanasia. In Chapter 3, I explain the methods used to identify and document clinical cases of euthanasia, and the limits of my methodology. The twenty-six cases gathered from my fieldwork are reprinted at the end of the chapter. In Chapter 4, I develop an evaluative scheme (based on the criteria used by the Dutch themselves) to analyze the individual cases. Specifically, my concern in this chapter is to examine how the presumed limits of euthanasia manifest themselves in individual cases and how the clinicians who practice euthanasia understand and rationalize the guidelines under which it is permitted.

In Chapter 5, the conclusion, I return again to the regulatory question and suggest several problems with both the implementation and the theory of the existing regulatory controls in the Netherlands. Moreover, I suggest to those who will determine the American response to physician-assisted suicide that at least insofar as euthanasia is concerned, the Dutch experience might better serve as a cautionary tale than as a paradigm worthy of emulation.

—— *Acknowledgments* ——

In carrying out a complicated project of this sort, numerous institutions and people have been of invaluable help to me. These pages are inadequate to the debt I owe—and to the gratitude I feel—but they will have to suffice for the moment.

It was under the auspices, and with the financial support, of the Pew Program in Medicine, the Arts, and the Social Sciences that I had the good fortune to come to the University of Chicago in 1986. The trustees of the Pew Memorial Fund and the Pew Charitable Trusts have my thanks for supporting this unique program, as does the University of Chicago, for the institution's open-mindedness and hospitality to such a project. To Dr. Godfrey Getz, the founder of the program and original director; to Dr. Stanley Yachnin, his successor; and to Roberta Siegal, administrative assistant to the Pew Program: dreams sometimes do come true. Thank you for both creating and directing such an enterprise and for letting me be a part of it.

At the University of Chicago, I was fortunate to have four faculty members direct this project as part of my work toward a doctorate from the Graduate School of Public Policy Studies. Christine K. Cassel, M.D., was a gracious and generous mentor. She encouraged and aided this project from its inception and urged me to pursue this research no matter where it led. Leon R. Kass, M.D., asked the questions no one else had thought of and provided a remarkable example of how a physician and teacher can pursue excellence on several levels. Edward F. Lawlor, Ph.D., anticipated problems with this research early on and helped me to correct them long before they became insurmountable. Steve H. Miles, M.D., was my best and most severe critic. He taught me to think *and* feel through these problems in medicine, "because we owe it to our patients." This study is a better product because of his participation; I hope I am a better doctor for having known Steve. To all who helped guide me through the thinking and writing of this study—and to my other teachers at Chicago—thank you.

At the University of Virginia Medical School, I have had the good fortune to find a community of welcoming and supportive faculty and friends, who have encouraged me in this—and many other—enterprises. My thanks in particular go to Kenneth R. Crispell, M.D., Oscar A. Thorup, M.D.; James F. Childress, Ph.D.; and Julian N. Hartt, Ph.D.

Erwin Glikes, president and publisher of The Free Press, first suggested that my private concerns about euthanasia might have a larger public audience. I thank him for the suggestion and for the confidence he expressed in my work. My thanks also go to Noreen O'Connor and the rest of the editorial staff at the Free Press for their unflagging patience and good counsel.

My family has been my joy throughout this project, and in my worst of times (for this *is* a grim topic), they taught me to cast my "awful solemnity to the winds, and join in the General Dance." I thank them. My wife, Mimi, listened to and critiqued this topic more times than she or I care to remember, and she encouraged my original application to Chicago. Our daughter, Madeleine, was a young (but hardy) traveler to the Netherlands. I wrote this study with her; she was literally, at times, on my back. As she has grown, so have her father's preoccupations and outside obligations. I ask her indulgence in these matters that are so important to me, and I thank her in particular for the cries and laughter that reminded me of what was truly important. It is to Madeleine that I dedicate this work.

— 1 —

Introduction:
The Limits
of a Public Death

Here is to the world that goes
round on wheels
Death is a thing that all man feels
If death was a thing
that the rich could buy
The rich would live
and the poor would die.[1]

DEATH IN A MEDICAL CONTEXT

How should we die? It is a question that assumes that humans have some control over the manner—if not the time and circumstance—of their deaths. At one end of human possibilities, it is a question that for many has been purely theoretical. Accidents of one sort or another, wars, and unforeseen and lethal illnesses all temper and to some extent negate the importance of the question. In these circumstances, we can ponder and meditate, but ultimately we have little or no control over our end. At the opposite extreme, there are the lucky,[2] who die a late, quiet death, what some call a "natural death,"[3] free from extreme pain, without complete loss of dignity, for whom the passage from life seems relatively easeful. They die, as it were, under their own power, when life seems simply to have run out.

In between, however, lie the vast majority of people in this country and, indeed, in most of the industrialized Western world. This "halfway" place, which most of us will or currently occupy, seems to

1

have become the province of medical care and of the physicians, nurses, and other medical workers who render that care. It is the type of death, for example, that comes after strenuous, even excessive, efforts to stave it off. It comes in spite of drugs, diets, and therapeutic protocols. It comes during or after surgeries, in the midst of procedures. It comes with plastic bottles and tubes attached to individuals, with machines that help people breathe or filter impurities from the blood. It is the type of death where pain is sometimes tempered by analgesics and narcotics. It is the type of death that is charted and noted, discussed and analyzed, by people who are usually strangers and who may enter the person's life precisely at (or close to) the time of the person's death. It is the type of death that occurs, generally, outside of the home. It happens in hospitals and nursing homes and (much less often) hospices. It is an institutional type of death.

The word "institutional" in this context needs to be further expanded, for it is central to the discussions that follow. The term, as first construed, refers to locality, the place where people die. That most people die outside of the home is, in itself, a major cultural shift, one with serious implications for the dying person.[4] It places the locus of death away from an accustomed environment. Family and friends may visit and attend to the patient, but they generally have to do so in a tightly circumscribed manner. Moreover, what they may or may not do for the patient is also controlled. Drugs, for example, may be administered only by licensed personnel; visiting hours (and the number of visitors) are restricted. The particularities of the dying patient's household, with its familiar rhythm and customs, fall away, and the person's progress toward death is marked by schedules and routines not of their choosing and generally beyond their control.[5] And because these institutions are public (that is, outside of the home), the dying person often dies in the company of other strangers who themselves are dying. Save for the wealthy, who can command enough resources to create a more private space within this public environment, the typical person dying in an institution dies joined to the healings and deaths of unknown people.[6]

The institutional quality of death in the modern world also extends beyond the physical structure of the buildings where people practice medicine. It has to include the institutional aspects of the profession of medicine itself, characteristics of the profession as a whole that defy easy categorization. Many see the practice of medicine from anthropological and sociological perspectives.[7] The practice of medicine from these vantage points looks much like other organized human enterprises and is subject to being parsed with the same analytic tools. Thus, physicians and their practices may share characteristics of entrepreneurs, dominating elites, or private guilds.[8] The extent to which these organizational images of physicians are correct or even complete is debatable,[9] but it is important for our later discussions to note that others have construed the practice of medicine this way.

The institutional ethos of people who call themselves physicians adds another layer of complexity to this description. This particular aspect of institutionalism is in some sense harder to characterize, in part because there seems to be less and less public agreement—even within the profession—as to what defines the boundaries of professional conduct and what *within* those boundaries is essential to the proper practice of medicine.[10] Nevertheless, there is an institutional quality to the practice of medicine in this country, at least to the extent that there are standard and widely applied curricula in the schools and hospitals in which physicians train. The standardization of the education and training of physicians means that there is a shared body of knowledge over which all doctors need to demonstrate some level of mastery and competence. Multiple examinations, license requirements, and set lengths of residency, for example, all attest to an attempt to maintain some uniformity and minimum quality among the people who practice medicine. Paul Starr amplifies this idea in discussing the post-Flexnerian reforms of medical education in this country at the turn of the century:

> The new system greatly increased the homogeneity and cohesiveness of the profession. The extended period of training helped to instill common values and beliefs among doctors and the uniformity of the medical curriculum discouraged sectarian divisions. Under the old system of apprenticeships with solo practitioners, doctors acquired more idiosyncratic views of medicine and formed personal attachments with their preceptors rather than their peers. Hospital internships generated a stronger sense of shared identity among contemporaries.[11]

Starr's comment points to something deeper about the ethos of medicine. He notes that what began as a regulatory reform—an effort to drive out the quackery and charlatanism rampant in nineteenth-century American medicine—had the unforeseen consequence of creating what he above calls the "shared identity" of physicians. The acquisition of a common body of knowledge and technique, gained over several years from a shared group of tutors, led to "common values and beliefs." Those same values and beliefs not only governed the types of therapies and medical interventions employed[12] but also informed more subtle aspects of medical practice, such as when, if ever, patients should be told that their disease is fatal.

The multiplicity of formal and informal mechanisms at work today, then, suggest that what I above called "institutional death" is a decidedly complicated phenomenon. Death—that event to which we all will someday succumb—may overtake us in a variety of ways, and its approach may vary wildly from individual to individual. Yet when this most personal of events occurs in a medical context, there are aspects of it that pass beyond the control of the dying individual to professionals and their institutional mores.

PUBLIC AND PRIVATE DEATHS

Something about the transformation of the dying process should strike us as paradoxical. What was for centuries an essentially private matter is now an event that for many of us is mediated by institutions subject to public control and regulation: the very professional and charitable institutions that control medicine and medical care in this country are, themselves, subject to external control.[13]

For example, medical licensure is not only a form of professional control over entry into the profession itself but also a public declaration that people who practice medicine are themselves subject to some form of external oversight. At this most elemental level, it points to a sense of public accountability. Thus, physicians who willingly harm or deceive patients may lose their licenses (in addition to whatever other legal penalties the law applies in such cases). Similarly, the licensing of medical facilities, from tertiary-care hospitals to nursing homes, is also a public statement of the mission and standards of those institutions. A variety of formal legal and regulatory mechanisms impose standards, the violation of which may result in penalties. Hospitals, nursing homes, and other health care institutions that routinely violate standards may face disciplinary actions ranging from fines to forfeiture of license.[14] Thus, the public nature of both medicine and the institutions where medicine is practiced limits the scope and range of activities.

The evolution of public interest in and control over institutional deaths in this country has been slow and tortuous. Its trajectory reflects, to some extent, both the ambivalence of public institutions toward intrusion into what was traditionally a private affair and the resistance of medical professionals to regulation by nonmedical authorities. Perhaps more importantly, this incremental approach to regulation betrays ambiguous and conflicting sentiments over what constitutes proper medical care of the dying. In the therapeutic enthusiasm following the end of World War II—when American medicine seemed to offer remedies for countless maladies—few took note of, or exception to, potential problems or burdens that technical wizardry could bring. The introduction to resuscitative therapies for patients who had suffered a cardiac arrest is illustrative:

> The simultaneous introduction of defibrillation, mouth-to-mouth ventilation, and external cardiac massage in the late 1950s transformed the hospital management of sudden death. Cardiac arrest teams, mobile carts for resuscitation equipment, coronary care units, and nurses trained in defibrillation techniques quickly followed in the early and middle 1960s. . . . The medical community immediately recognized that cardiopulmonary resuscitation (CPR), which was developed as a therapy for unexpected cessation of cardiorespiratory function, was a unique kind of therapy.[15]

Many patients who would otherwise have died as the result of cardiac arrest were successfully resuscitated using these new techniques. A series of national consensus panels, which set standards for this new therapy, proposed in 1974 that health care institutions design protocols allowing their personnel (including nonphysicians) to initiate CPR without waiting for a physician's formal orders.[16]

This therapeutic "triumphalism" gave way, eventually, to more sobering critiques that called to task the unquestioning endorsement of medical intervention. The same medical technique that can literally restart the stopped circulation of a young woman following an unexpected cardiac arrest can also prolong the pain of an older patient with cancer as he dies a halting death, its inevitable progression punctuated by the starts and stops of life-sustaining therapies. The medical intervention may be identical in both cases, but its effect on the patient's condition is beneficial and welcome to one, burdensome and intrusive to another.

The skepticism with which new medical interventions were greeted—especially interventions that could somewhat alter the pace, but not the ultimate trajectory, of a dying patient's course—found expression in a variety of quarters. For example, articles in professional journals began to appear that challenged the unexamined use of medical technologies, especially when those interventions occurred without the clear consent of the patient. A prestigious presidential commission, established in 1978, issued a report suggesting limits on the use of such technologies and, what is more important, asserted the primacy of a patient's consent irrespective of the decision to treat or not to treat.[17] The President's commission—as well as a spate of well-publicized "right-to-die" court decisions—confirmed a growing sense that these matters are not properly under the exclusive control of the medical profession. More generally, what is prior and central to the resolution of these issues is the patient's private discretion in them. Nevertheless, this enhanced sense of patient autonomy over medical decisions also acknowledges the importance of public limits and of public or state interest in these matters.

Morris Abram, who chaired the President's commission, points to these overlapping areas of public and private interest: "Now most deaths in the United States occur in institutional settings, and for almost any life-threatening condition there is some intervention capable of delaying the moment of death. . . . Individual and institutional scrutiny of medical decision making is unavoidable."[18] Abram captures well the sense that even if there are overlapping areas of concern, one still properly defers to the judgment of the individuals most affected by the decisions: "Individuals should be able to make choices about medical care consistent with their personal morality and preferences."[19]

Abram's comments, however, are found in an article that attempts to defend (and limit) a role for public scrutiny and regulation in matters concerning death and dying. Even if one cedes a large portion of this area to individuals and their physicians, there is an appropriate role for some public presence in this private space. Abram continues: "At the same time, there is a case for some government involvement. Public participation is necessary for both political and pragmatic reasons. . . . Some of the most pressing issues are intrinsically collective and public."[20]

Thus, while it has become generally agreed that the state should help to promote and extend the rights of patients to choose or decline treatment, the state's neutrality on the substance of these choices, suggests Abram, cannot become total silence. Private acts can have public consequences. More particularly, private acts that involve public institutions—the physicians themselves and the establishments in which they work—necessarily have public limits.

If the collective sense is that private judgment should be given as wide a berth as possible in matters concerning death and dying, there has also been—at least until quite recently—a fairly sharp line demarcating the boundaries of private discretion, limiting the extent to which individuals can claim a right to an institution's aid in dying. Specifically, while patients can refuse or withdraw from particular interventions, there are some interventions on which they can make no positive claim. One of these prohibited interventions is the administration or proffering of a lethal drug to patients who request such. So-called "active" euthanasia or "assistance with suicide" has yet to find sanction in law and, to varying degrees of uniformity, still meets with disapprobation within the medical community.[21]

THE POLICY CONTEXT OF ETHICS IN MEDICINE: THREE EXAMPLES

What role should public policy play in matters concerning death and dying? Whatever private sentiments and beliefs inform one's position on euthanasia, one has to attend to the problem of a public voice on it. I have suggested earlier that the private question of how one should die necessarily engages larger civic responsibilities. My approach to this particular aspect of euthanasia has been shaped by an exercise in policy analysis that has its nearer and more recent origins in a separate, but related, question: to what extent should public policy in the United States shape the right of patients to refuse or to withdraw from life-sustaining treatments?

During the summer of 1987, the Office of Technology Assessment (OTA), which is constituted as an advisory body to the U.S. Congress, contracted with a group at the University of Chicago to prepare a document outlining what appropriate role institutional protocols might play in helping to guide patients and clinicians in making these difficult decisions. The document, which underwent several revisions after review by a national panel of experts, was published by Congress the following year.[22] As a member of the group that researched and wrote the original study, I was struck by a number of aspects of the project.

I was impressed, for example, that so private and difficult a matter as establishing decision-making guidelines on when to discontinue life-sustaining medical treatment had come under the scrutiny of this country's highest legislative body. The question that seemed noteworthy to me was not *whether* the government should comment or legislate on this problem, but *how*.

Take, as one example, the so-called Baby Doe regulations. Former Surgeon General C. Everett Koop's attempt to institutionalize these rules in federally supported hospitals fell prey to strong resistance from organized professional groups and was eventually defeated.[23] Even many who were sympathetic to aims of the regulations—that handicapped newborns not be denied treatment (as a matter of course) because of their handicap—objected to what was perceived as a clumsy intrusion by the government into matters requiring a more sensitive exercise of judgment and prudence.[24] Although the intent was to protect the lives of a particularly vulnerable and needy group of patients, the government's heavy-handed approach became counterproductive and was eventually deemed unconstitutional by the U.S. Supreme Court.[25]

If the sentiment here was that the government's efforts were inappropriately intrusive, however, another case of governmental oversight suggests the dangers of too lax a regulatory standard. In 1982, the Health Care Financing Administration (HCFA) published a preliminary set of rules that would have allowed nursing homes to seek certification from a nongovernmental organization. Specifically, HCFA proposed that nursing homes be allowed to seek accreditation through the Joint Commission on Accreditation of Hospitals (JCAH) as an alternative to certification through state or federal agencies.[26] HCFA defended the rules as an attempt to simplify a complex and relatively ineffective set of regulatory guidelines, in the hope, it said, of bringing greater efficiency to the nursing home industry.[27] Another consequence of HCFA's new scheme, however, would have been that responsibility for certification—which makes a health care facility eligible for certain public funds—could potentially have passed from a public to a private agency. More importantly, not only would the disbursement of public funds fall, in a fashion, into private hands, but also one of the few public sanctions available to control the quality of nursing homes would have been removed. The strong dissent registered by certain lay and professional groups brought sufficient political pressure to bear on HCFA that the agency was forced to back down from its original position. Those who protested most vigorously (the advocacy groups for the disabled and the aged, for example) felt that the government was shunting a public responsibility— protection of vulnerable citizens—to private quarters.[28] Demented patients, young people with severe physical or mental disabilities, and indigent elderly forced by declining health to seek care outside of their homes were all seen as particularly susceptible to abuse without the benefit of some public accountability.

The tension between public oversight and private discretion represented by these two extreme cases manifested itself again in the proceedings surrounding the OTA report on life-sustaining treatments. At a conference convened to review the preliminary report, the directors of the OTA project invited several people representing a variety of perspectives on this matter. The criticisms of some people representing the interests of nursing home residents (who suggested that the preliminary draft gave scant attention to dangers that termination-of-treatment protocols might represent for these people), for example, were challenged by others, who pointed to a substantial body of case law that gave substantial weight to patient autonomy and discretion in this area. Along similar lines, representatives from organized medical and hospital groups were concerned that whatever consensus emerged about the desirability of institutional protocols should not be couched in language that might invite (or demand) further government regulation of professional or corporate conduct in medical care. Thus, while admitting to a certain attractiveness to institutional statements on termination-of-treatment guidelines, these groups also strongly urged that professional discretion not be undercut by government mandate.[29]

How to incorporate the competing claims and interests of these different groups in a public document was a problem that the final version of the OTA report addressed with varying degrees of success. The limited success of such an enterprise stems from various factors. One, clearly, is the very nature of the subject. There was an appropriate reluctance on the part of a public agency to stipulate rigid criteria for evaluating ethical dilemmas that are ambiguous and contingent on the particulars of these difficult cases.[30] Moreover, there was a proper regard for the need to protect the privacy and latitude that have historically characterized the range of decisions made within a medical context. Ethical judgments made from too far a distance—especially those made from behind the safe and anonymous screen of bureaucratic regulations—often do violence to the very people who are the object of such concern.[31]

As I suggested earlier, however, these private decisions play themselves out against the backdrop of larger public concerns and interests. Not only do public monies play a role in helping to support almost the entire edifice of medical care in this country (which, in itself, might be justification for government regulation), but also the state's interest in protecting its citizens—especially the weakest and most vulnerable among us—finds legitimate expression in its concern over protocols that guide how and when patients and physicians decide to end life-sustaining treatments.[32] Any one of us may have particular and well-justified reasons for seeking or declining medical treatment that might sustain our existence, but our private inclinations need at least *some* public expression and justification when our wishes make claims on the offices of a particular profession (such as medicine) or when our actions play themselves out within an institution (such as a hospital) designed to attend to the needs of others besides ourselves. Said differently, a private claim on a public good, however appropriate, needs a fuller justification than is contained in a simple expression of preference.[33] At the very least, we have to demonstrate that our claim does not interfere with the equally valid claims of others on the good or, alternatively, that by meeting our private claim, a public institution does not diminish or damage its ability to serve the broader needs of others.

Thus, for example, the criticism that some advocates for the disabled level against termination-of-treatment protocols is born, in part, of a fear that the interests of vulnerable patients will be compromised by making withdrawal of life-sustaining medical care too routine, so that the presumption in difficult cases moves from treatment to nontreatment. Although a presumption is not decisive in these matters, it may have the effect of shifting the burden of the argument onto those patients least able to articulate and advance their claim to continued medical care. At the same time, to make the justification for termination of treatment so exceptional a practice or so elaborate or contentious a process (via court petitions, for example) forces a public institution to intrude into areas where it is clearly not wanted and where it can do nothing but further harm. Some patients do decline treatments, others withdraw from treatment, and still others never seek treatment for whatever lesion threatens to kill them. They make either no claim or a limited claim on the good that the institution of medicine might be able to provide. To force a public "good" on these patients (in an effort to protect others) is, in a very literal sense, to do violence to them.[34]

Even if the resolution of this particular issue in medicine and public policy fails to satisfy fully, it is instructive on other points and suggests a way of analyzing the growing calls for euthanasia legislation in this country. It understates the case to say that this exercise in policy formation demonstrates the difficulty in crafting the public limits on matters as complex as these. It also suggests that, by their very nature, policy statements on ethical conduct in medicine fail to meet fully the needs of all people the policy aims to serve, partly because they do not capture the subtleties of individual cases, and partly because some needs (or desires) of different individuals resist being publicly reconciled to one another.[35]

Most importantly, perhaps, it suggests that translating broadly stated principles of medical ethics into practice—implementing policy aims into a program of specific action—is a decidedly delicate process, laden with unforeseen problems and dangers, some of which I described above. The notion that patients who are suffering as they approach their deaths should be a special object of our concern is an appropriate, even noble, goal; said that way, it is unobjectionable. To move from that goal to a specific recommendation that the "specialness" of these patients' condition justifies creating a new practice that would allow them to seek death via a physician's administration of a poison, however, moves us back into the problemmatic terrain of policy implementation.[36] In the following section, I review the arguments on both sides of this issue, in an effort to translate the debate into terms more useful to the development of guidelines.

THE CURRENT DEBATE

The controversy in the United States surrounding the practice of euthanasia has been, until quite recently, of an abstract and speculative nature. Although various groups throughout the twentieth century have called for legalization of euthanasia, they have generally failed to mount a serious challenge to existing laws and medical custom and have been uniformly unsuccessful.[37]

During the past few years, however, the controversy has taken on topical importance. Various groups, most notably the Hemlock Society, helped draft a statute called the Humane and Dignified Death Act (HDDA), which would have permitted physicians in California to euthanize patients who were terminally ill and who requested the procedure.[38] Although the proponents of this measure failed to obtain enough signatures to place it on the state ballot in November 1988, it represented the most serious challenge to date of laws prohibiting the intentional killing of patients by physicians in this country. Moreover, the leader of the legislative movement vowed to try anew.[39] Similar challenges to existing practices are expected this year in Oregon, and Proposition 119 (which would decriminalize physician-assisted suicide) will be put to a vote in November in the State of Washington.[40]

A few months before the HDDA proposition failed, the *Journal of the American Medical Association* (JAMA) published "It's Over, Debbie," an anonymous (and possibly apocryphal) article, in which a physician described euthanizing a young patient who had cancer.[41] The article generated a storm of controversy. Some protested not only the alleged actions of the physician in question but the very act of publishing (without editorial comment) such an article—which in essence described the commission of a homicide—in so prestigious a journal.[42] Others—though taking exception to particular details of the case—applauded the fact that the debate over this practice was finally being made public.[43]

Most recently, a retired pathologist, Dr. Jack Kevorkian, assisted in the suicide of a 54-year-old woman suffering from Alzheimer's disease, who wanted to end her life before she deteriorated further. Dr. Kevorkian's participation in this woman's death consisted of connecting her, via an intravenous line, to a machine that would dispense solutions from three vials. The first vial contained saline; the other two contained thiopental (a barbiturate) and potassium chloride. After Kevorkian instructed her in the use of the machine—and with Kevorkian looking on—the woman, in essence, injected herself with the lethal substances and quickly died.[44]

Kevorkian, who notified local authorities in Michigan of his actions, was enjoined from further use of the machine. Moreover, murder charges were brought against him, which were subsequently dismissed by a Michigan judge, who noted that neither suicide nor assistance with suicide were illegal in the state of Michigan. Although the injunction against the use of Dr. Kevorkian's machine remains in place—and other lesser charges may still be brought against Kevorkian—the ruling in the case was widely applauded by those in the United States who now see an opening for assistance with suicide by medical professionals.[45]

To proponents of euthanasia in the United States, the events of the past two years are part of a slow and much-needed progression toward greater patient control over decisions affecting their medical care, a course that they believe should culminate in the right of terminally ill patients to receive assistance from physicians in committing suicide Some have argued that this movement takes origin from a better-informed public that has wrested control from a dominating, paternalistic profession.[46] Others have suggested that the dramatic advances in exotic life-sustaining technologies have left many people, especially the elderly and those with some degenerative diseases (for example, amyotrophic lateral sclerosis), apprehensive that control over the natural progression of their diseases will pass to a machine.[47] The call for respect for patient autonomy in these medical decisions, it is argued, is in part a response to this fear.

Whatever the historical roots of this call for enhanced patient autonomy, it undoubtedly has changed the environment in which medicine is practiced. As noted above, hospitals, nursing homes, and other institutions providing medical care have responded by establishing protocols that specifically endorse the principle of patient autonomy in refusing or withdrawing from medical treatment.[48] Moreover, professional organizations have issued similar statements.[49] The opinions of the courts (the earliest and most famous of which was *In re Quinlan*, in 1976) and of ethicists have further advanced and supported this position.[50]

These developments point to a convergence of opinion among professional groups, the courts, and the general public; something of a consensus, then, seems to have developed in this particular area of public policy. Although there still remain areas of contention and serious disagreement (for example, whether artificial feeding and hydration represent medical treatment or attention to basic human needs), it is essential to note that the responses of every professional organization, as well as the opinions of the courts, have stopped short of endorsing a presumed right on the part of patients to be euthanized. In other language, while current policy says that patients may choose to refuse or withdraw from a particular type of treatment, that freedom of choice does not include enlisting the aid of a physician in committing suicide.

It was in this environment that the Humane and Dignified Death Act failed and in which the controversy surrounding "It's Over, Debbie" raged. Those who supported passage of the HDDA in California claimed that the measure failed because they lacked sufficient resources to mount a thorough campaign and because their proposal was misrepresented by the medical profession, notably the California Medical Association (CMA). Derek Humphrey, president of the Hemlock Society, went even further, charging that the CMA's opposition was "hypocritical" because Dr. Laurens White, the association's president, was on record as having recommended suicide to a number of patients and had even "given them prescriptions to do so, telling them what dosages to take."[51] Dr. White did not deny Humphrey's charges, but he replied with the curious defense that he opposed active euthanasia because "I don't want to do it myself. I don't want to pull the trigger."[52] Humphrey characterized White's rationalization as "phony," claiming that prescribing a lethal dosage of a medication for a patient as opposed to injecting the patient himself was a distinction without a difference.

The recent exchange between Humphrey and White is a distorted echo of an older argument between those who oppose active euthanasia (though for reasons dramatically different from Dr. White's) and those who see it as a beneficent and appropriate form of treatment for the terminally ill. Moreover, the debate following the failure of the HDDA proposal points to two important aspects of the problem that lie at the heart of this study.

Killing, Letting Die, and the Ethos of Medicine

Proponents of active euthanasia have argued that the distinction between allowing a terminal patient to die (by withholding treatment, by withdrawing treatment) and causing or hastening a patient's death through a physician's direct and intended intervention lacks moral force.[53] The ultimate result of both practices, they argue, is the same, though they make the further claim that actively ending a suffering patient's life is a more humane (and, therefore, more praiseworthy) approach. Opponents of active euthanasia have argued that a moral distinction does, in fact, exist, and they have made this point from both secular and theological perspectives.[54]

For the policy questions to be addressed in this study, however, there is an even more important objection raised by opponents of physician-assisted suicide: namely, it lies outside the established ethic of medical practice.[55] Killing one's patients—however noble the intentions—is outside the "physician's frame of reference" (to borrow Albert Jonsen's phrase). Leaving aside the question of whether *other* members of society might assume the role of euthanists, some opponents of physician-assisted suicide note that the prohibition against killing is embedded within the Hippocratic Oath and is part of the ethos intrinsic to the proper practice of medicine.[56] Thus, a change that would allow physicians to kill their patients—even within the most tightly controlled circumstances—would not be a mere addition to the physician's techniques and drugs. Rather, it would fundamentally alter that established "frame of reference."

At the heart of this matter is a question that points to the role of physicians in society. To the extent that a society perceives a profession to be self-regulating, beneficent, honest, and its activities efficacious and consistent, society accords that profession particular status within a culture. What in one context is battery upon a person becomes a thorough (and appropriate) physical examination within the ethos of medical practice.[57] Moreover, the privileges of privacy and confidentiality that currently attend the encounter between a physician and a patient are a further expression of societal trust that physicians and the medical profession do not abuse that privilege (at least not on an extensive or regular basis). Were this not the case—were we as patients completely cynical or suspicious about the motives that lie behind physician practices—our approach to the medical encounter would be more tentative and might include the proviso that a third party observe and evaluate the encounter. (I note here as an aside that this already occurs in the various reimbursement regulatory reforms enacted in the 1970s and 1980s; what I mean to suggest is a further erosion of trust, so that even the *physical* encounter between patient and physician would be subject to the scrutiny of regulatory eyes.) Those who oppose physician-assisted suicide point precisely to this erosion of public trust and additionally suggest that sanctioning physician-assisted suicide will further erode that trust.[58]

Professional Virtue and Societal Regulation

Proponents of active euthanasia in the United States suggest that sanctioning physicians-assisted suicide will not further erode physician-patient trust because it is a practice that would be tightly and effectively controlled, and they point to the experience with this practice in the Netherlands.[59] One commentator, though applauding publication of "It's Over, Debbie," objected to the *process* described in the article and further claimed that the actions of the physician in question would have led to prosecution and conviction in the Netherlands.[60] Moreover, other proponents of this measure suggest that it is precisely in the absence of societal controls that abuses of the practice of physician-assisted suicide occur. The documented cases of "mercy killings" over the last two decades point to a societal desire for this practice, and the appropriate professional response would be to accommodate this desire and subsume the practice of euthanasia under the ethic of medical practice.[61]

Those who oppose physician-assisted suicide practice suggest precisely the opposite. The appropriate response of the profession should not *always* be to accommodate societal desires (however sincere), especially when they remain open to abuses. Of particular concern are those patients least able to advance or defend their interests in society, namely, the very old, the disabled, the mentally handicapped, and the socially stigmatized.[62] If this practice is allowed for cognitively intact patients, what is to prevent its being extended to the confused and inarticulate? Would not this practice, in fact, encourage something like a coarsening of the spirit of medicine, so that what begins as a small circle of select patients—terminally ill, cognitively intact, and in unbearable pain—widens progressively to include other categories of patients?[63] Regulations, however cunningly designed, depend at least to *some* extent on the acceptance and goodwill of those being regulated. Would not this practice eventually diminish an acceptance of regulatory limits and, in fact, encourage our darker impulses (such as those that are alleged in critiques of "It's Over, Debbie")?

THE NETHERLANDS AS A PARADIGM

It strikes me that the arguments of both sides of this issue in the United States are being played out, in rough fashion, in an experiment of sorts in the Netherlands. Since approximately 1973, the Dutch have allowed physicians, under particular circumstances, to end the lives of patients who request assistance with suicide. The defense and acceptance of such a practice in the Netherlands, moreover, broadly parallels the arguments of those who would allow euthanasia in the United States, and provides several points of comparison.

The reasoning of those in the United States who defend the acceptability of euthanasia on the principle of a patient's freedom to choose, for example, is almost perfectly realized in the Dutch interpretation of permissible euthanasia. There is an appeal to patient autonomy, for example, which has been given such weight in the Netherlands that the courts have found other competing interests insufficient to override a request for euthanasia. Thus, claims that euthanasia lies outside the ethic of medical practice or that it creates unjustifiable dangers for certain categories of patients have been subordinated to what is seen as the overriding right of patients to seek their end through a medical practice.[64]

There is, moreover, a well-established sentiment in the Netherlands that parallels another argument of those who would decriminalize euthanasia in the United States: there is no distinction between withdrawing life-sustaining medical intervention during the agonal stages of a patient's illness and killing the patient outright. Thus, the Dutch have dispensed with the terms *active* and *passive* euthanasia, and use the term *euthanasia,* simply and exclusively, to denote a physician's intentional killing of a patient at the patient's express request.

The notion that the practice of euthanasia is one that the medical profession can safely incorporate into accepted standards of care, furthermore, receives support from organized medicine in the Netherlands. The Royal Dutch Society for the Promotion of Medicine (KNMG) has adopted euthanasia as a permissible medical practice. In fact, it has drawn up guidelines on the practice, with the intent of instructing its member physicians on acceptable limits of euthanasia, as well as on the medical specifics of the procedure. The KNMG was also instrumental in lending support to the euthanasia movement in the Netherlands, by intervening on behalf of physicians accused of homicide for practicing euthanasia, for example, and by testifying before government commissions on the desirability of the practice from a medical standpoint.

The Dutch position on euthanasia, thus, not only recapitulates many of the justifications for the practice found in this country, but it also captures many of the same tensions discussed earlier between private needs or desires and public duties. Without enshrining in written law the right to euthanasia, the Dutch courts have crafted an opening for the practice. They have also found, however, that the public responsibility for protecting vulnerable patients against the abuse of an unwanted and untimely death at the hands of physicians sits uncomfortably with the now-accepted right of Dutch citizens to obtain euthanasia. Through a variety of legal, political, and professional actions, the Dutch have tried to reconcile this newly discovered right with older customs and practices designed to distinguish medicine as a healing, not a killing, practice.

The extent to which the Dutch have been able to succeed in this task is the subject of the next three chapters in this study. I examine the role of the courts, the legislature, and the medical profession in trying to regulate the practice. Although there is no perfect symmetry between the United States and the Netherlands, the policy questions engendered by the American debate may be partially answered through this study. Although the regulatory process I will describe is sometimes ambiguous and conflicting, it raises the same issues of professional virtue, professional control, and societal demands for a particular change. Moreover, the practice seems to be well enough established for us to begin to see at least the outlines of how such change might be played should euthanasia be sanctioned in the United States.

The larger and more important question of whether or not the practice of euthanasia is intrinsically benign or evil deserves (and has received) attention from other quarters. My effort here is to try to document the details of this practice in the Netherlands and to analyze the policy implications. Given the current state of affairs, it is an effort that may help to sharpen the focus of a controversy that will surely overtake Americans again in the near future.

— 2 —

Euthanasia as a Public Matter: Legal, Political, and Professional Aspects of Control

He who robs another of life at his express and serious wish is punished with a prison sentence of at most twelve years or a fine of the fifth category.[1]

He who deliberately incites another to suicide, assists him therein or provides him with the means is punished, if the suicide follows, with a prison sentence of at most three years or a fine of the fourth category.[2]

THE FORMAL LIMITS OF EUTHANASIA

The intentional killing of a patient by a physician—or, for that matter, the killing of any person by another—is illegal in the Netherlands. Yet every commentator on the practice of physician-assisted suicide in the Netherlands argues that it occurs with regularity[3] and that physicians are rarely prosecuted and even more rarely punished.[4] How does one reconcile this apparent contradiction between the laws prohibiting killing and the well-established practice of euthanasia in the Netherlands?[5] If the laws seem antiquated or seem to frustrate prevailing public and professional sentiment on this subject, why have they not been changed?[6]

19

The practice of euthanasia in the Netherlands exists in a social context of significant tension. It is a practice that—though seemingly well-embedded in the mainstream of medical practice—exists at the margins of the penal code, with marginal formal legal protection.[7] It is a practice that is still evolving, and whose specific limits continue to undergo revision and refinement.[8]

It is, moreover, a procedure that has insinuated itself into medical practice in the sense that euthanasia became established piecemeal—case by case—before becoming sanctioned and codified by the profession and the courts. Thus, policies and regulations have lagged behind the practice of euthanasia and have reacted to—rather than initiated—new developments in the practice. The constant modification of protocols and guidelines issued by the courts, professional organizations, and hospitals, for example, points to an attempt to respond on a continuing basis to unique characteristics of particular cases.[9]

What has emerged, then, over the last fifteen years or so that this matter has been adjudicated in the courts and debated in lay and professional circles is not a consistent set of policy rules.[10] Rather, what exists is a series of guidelines—in the form of court opinions, government commission statements, and hospital protocols—that attempt to refine the definition of euthanasia and establish the boundaries of its proper practice. Absent formal regulations, says Dr. Helene Dupuis, a Dutch ethicist who has written widely on the subject, the idea has been to create a "private place" within public policy where consenting patients may "seek relief in the form of a humane death" from physicians. Thus, she continues,

> we have a somewhat confusing situation because we want killing to remain illegal, but to provide a way for doctors to help patients who want to die quickly and without pain . . . and without the fear of being called murderers. It's not an easy thing doing this . . . how do you make such a law? Until then, we have not so formal rules that let doctors do their duty and hope they are protected.[11]

This idea of a "private place" or "private space" within public regulation is repeated often in discussions with the Dutch. It also resonates with many written commentaries on the subject of death and dying, both in the Netherlands and in more familiar English-language journals.[12]

The "private space" to which Dr. Dupuis and others refer is a shorthand expression that in many ways approximates what American jurisprudence has called "a right to privacy."[13] The term is meant—at least in this specific instance—to encompass an area where there is individual discretion in moral choice over death and dying. Although the ambiguous legal state of euthanasia has its distinct drawbacks, another Dutch ethicist points to what he sees as an advantage:

> Without saying so, we are telling people they have to be responsible, along with doctors, about this very difficult area. The courts can provide a limit, but [they] cannot say what happens within those limits. Some people and some doctors can believe euthanasia is immoral, and no one makes them do so. But for others, it may be the best solution . . . so the official policy is not to encourage and not to condemn [as long as] the guidelines are followed.[14]

This current arrangement, which tries to create an extralegal sphere of medical practice, relies heavily on at least two assumptions.

First, it places an immense amount of trust and discretion in the Dutch medical profession and the institutions it runs. It not only assumes an extremely high level of professional competence, expertise, and virtue, but it also assumes a high degree of uniformity and professional self-regulation. To permit such a practice under these circumstances suggests a remarkable confidence in the medical profession: that the practice will not be abused, that it will conform to guidelines, that physicians practicing euthanasia will act in the best interests of the patient. Absent this confidence, euthanasia would appear to even the most ardent of supporters to be a prescription for disaster.[15]

A second assumption (clearly related to the first) is that the boundaries of the private space within which doctor and patient make these decisions are well circumscribed and well policed. Thus, there must be some consensus about what constitutes exceptions to the legal prohibitions against killing. Moreover, there must also be some sense of the limits of the private space. What are the penalties, for example, for those who step beyond this private area? How does the physician, the patient, or the court, know when there has been transgression against the public interest in protecting the life of a citizen?

The first assumption regarding the regularity, conformity, and self-regulation of this practice within the medical profession is an evaluative question that receives considerable attention in the subsequent two chapters. Before we ask whether or not this convention between the public and the medical profession is well founded, however, we need a better sense of what the Dutch understand as the formal boundaries of the practice. In this chapter, I begin by describing what the Dutch intend when they speak of euthanasia. This exercise serves not only to lend some precision to subsequent discussions but also to give one an indication of how the Dutch perceive the need for controls on euthanasia.[16]

The elaborations on the language used to describe the practice serve as a useful preface to a more substantive discussion of the legal boundaries of the practice. I trace and comment upon a series of court cases that first created a public opening for acceptance of the practice of euthanasia in the Netherlands. I follow this with a discussion of the political and professional responses to these court initiatives. Finally, I conclude with a summary of the available evidence on the frequency and prevalence of the practice.

WHAT IS MEANT BY EUTHANASIA?

Do Dutch physicians practice euthanasia, mercy killing, medical killing, or assisted suicide? Does the terminology matter, or are all the words perfect synonyms, or do they at least describe the same practice from different vantage points?

In reviewing the Dutch literature on this practice—and in discussion with Dutch physicians, lawyers, and bioethicists—one is struck by the interchangeability of the words used to describe it.[17] One might initially suspect that the terminology reflects some ambiguity in the language or some confusion in translating from Dutch to English. Yet each word in Dutch has its near-perfect English counterpart, and it is the Dutch themselves (not their translators) who use these multiple terms.[18] Even official and quasi-official statements on the practice use various terms. For example, one report entered in parliamentary debate, entitled "Advies inzake Euthanasie" (Advice regarding Euthanasia), uses the terms *euthanasie, zelfdoding* (suicide), and *hulp bij zelfdoding* (assistance with suicide).[19] Others, especially some physicians whom I interviewed, prefer the term *assistance with death*. Fewer insist on the most active terms: *mercy killing* and *medical killing*. Those who insist on these latter terms are also the most publicly outspoken in defense of the practice and say that irrespective of what one calls the practice, the essence of the event remains the same.[20]

Another interpretation, one that seems more promising, is that the differing terminology reflects an unresolved tension either in this practice or in attempts to defend this practice.[21] The term *euthanasia* itself derives from a compound of two Greek words meaning "good death" (*eu* meaning "well" or "good," and *thanatos* meaning "death").

This term, however, does not denote or describe how one achieves a good death, nor the agent or agents responsible for a good death. It has, however, come to connote a shortening of the agonal stages before death and a relatively painless, easy passage into death. In modern Holland (and, indeed, in most commentaries on the subject) it also implies that the agent or coagent in the act is a physician.

The other terms employed to describe the practice are chosen to emphasize (or diminish) particular characteristics of the event. Thus, *hulp bij zelfdoding* (help with suicide) is a term that places the patient's wishes at the center of the event; the physician assists in or accedes to the patient's desire to die. What is central in the use of this particular term is the primacy of self-determination and patient autonomy; the physician's aid is seen as an expression of non-paternalistic intervention.[22] *Mercy killing* and *medical killing* are less often used because they employ the verb *to kill;* they also carry a good deal of painful historical baggage.[23] Although some American commentators (and some opponents of the practice) use these terms,[24] most of the Dutch jurists and bioethicists with whom I spoke eschew the terms because of their association with the barbarism of doctors in the Weimar Republic of Germany during the 1920s and the subsequent genocidal practices of the Nazis.[25] Moreover, the terms run counter to the current trend in medical ethics and jurisprudence to factor in most heavily a patient's desires in resolving ethical and legal disputes. Someone (the physician) has to be merciful in the term *mercy killing,* and it has the ring of a gift or dispensation that is within the physician's purview to give. Similarly, *medical killing* is something that doctors do, but the term says nothing about why or under what circumstances.

Thus, the fact that a variety of words and phrases are used to describe this practice reflects some of the tensions in current Dutch medical practice, and it would obscure (rather than relieve) that tension to settle invaryingly on one term in this study. Nevertheless, *euthanasia* is the term with most global acceptance, and it is the term I will use generally to describe this practice. *To euthanize* (though harsh sounding) is the verb derived from *euthanasia.* I will use the other terms mentioned above at specific times (especially when they occur in an interview or a case discussion) and when they illuminate a particular aspect of the practice.

This discussion of nomenclature, however, still fails to describe precisely what is meant by euthanasia in the Netherlands. It might be useful as a first step to discuss situations that seem related and have sometimes been confused with euthanasia. H. J. J. Leenen, a noted jurist at the University of Amsterdam and an advocate of changing the penal code to permit voluntary euthanasia, offers a summary of what he calls "distorted silhouettes of euthanasia." The justifications for these "silhouettes" seem to fall under four general categories: medical futility; double effect, or unintended side effect; patient autonomy in choosing to decline or withdraw from medical treatment; and scarcity of medical resources. Leenen's comments have gained wide currency in the Netherlands, and it is worth quoting a portion of his discussion in its entirety:

> *Termination of pointless treatment.* Medical treatment is justified by its sense, and the means used have to be proportional to the aim sought to be achieved. When a cure is no longer possible, no improvement can result from medical acts, and the available means are disproportionate, the doctor is then entitled to end the medical treatment. When a patient dies because of this decision, this is not regarded as euthanasia. Nobody is legally bound to do the impossible or to act unnecessarily. When medicine has nothing to offer, medical treatment becomes pointless. Decisions to terminate a medically pointless treatment may not include non-medical criteria or a judgement about the sense of a person's life: it is bound to within the limits of medical professional standards. When the notion of medically pointless treatment is extended with other than medical criteria, it loses its medical character. After the termination of the treatment, of course, normal care and sedation of pain have to be administered.
>
> *Painkilling.* The aim of palliation is to alleviate the patient's suffering. The possibility of thereby shortening the patient's life is a side-effect; the aim is not to terminate life. Acts must be defined not according to their side-effects, but according to their aim, which is to relieve the pain which the patient is suffering.
>
> *Refusal of medical treatment.* No patient may be treated without his consent, and it is his right to withdraw the given consent. Then the doctor is not entitled to treat. When the patient dies as a consequence of his refusal, the doctor has not administered euthanasia by omitting to act.
>
> *Force majeure.* A situation of "force majeure" (necessity) exists when a doctor is unable to treat all patients who request his help.[26] Then the decision to treat one patient may imply the death of another one. The doctor then does not administer euthanasia. Again, no one can be held responsible for the impossible.[27]

Euthanasia, says Leenen, is to be understood as "intentional life-termination by somebody other than the person concerned at the request of the latter. Assistance to suicide is at stake when the life-terminating act is performed by the suicidant with repeated requested assistance of another person, for instance, providing the means."[28] His definition follows directly from the Netherlands State Commission on Euthanasia report, issued in 1985.[29] Clearly, though, the instances in which "life-termination by somebody other than the person concerned" are excused have been confined to specific medical exceptions to Article 293 of the Penal Code. The evolution of those exceptions, and their acceptance as part of medical practice by professionals in the Netherlands, form part of the boundaries between the "private space" in Holland, where doctors and patients encounter each other, and the public limits of what may occur within that private encounter. The history of that legal reasoning, and the profession's translation of that reasoning, merit further attention.

THE COURTS AND EUTHANASIA: ADMONISH AND PARDON

All the legal rulings of the past two decades that have excused or pardoned physicians for practicing euthanasia have had to contend with the clear prohibitions of Article 293. They have had to find grounds on which the defendant may be excused, or his or her penalty lessened or pardoned, without doing violence to statutory law in the process. There is an irony here that is not lost on those who defend these exceptions:

> The article [293] was enacted precisely to discourage suicide by penalizing those who assisted [in the act]. The reformers of the late nineteenth century wanted some rule that was less severe [than the] punishment for murder or manslaughter, but they wanted a rule. And here we are, arguing exceptions to a rule made to cover exceptions! It's not a very rational situation, is it?[30]

Others have also agreed that the legislative intent behind these statutes is to distinguish assisting in suicide from murder (by lessening the penalty for the former) while still discouraging assistance with suicide. Thus, "the lawgiver in Article 293 (killing upon serious and deliberate wish) did not abrogate punishment, but formulated grounds for diminishing punishment by comparison to murder or killing."[31]

This commentary goes on to quote at length from the explanatory memorandum attached to the original bill:

> He who accedes to another's expressed and serious wish to deprive himself of life deserves considerably less punishment than one who is guilty of ordinary murder. The assent cannot abrogate the criminalization [sic] of taking of a life, but [can] have it a wholly different character. The laws as it were no longer punishes the attack against the life of a particular person, but the violation of the respect which is due human life in general, regardless of the motive of the perpetrator. Crime against life remains, the attack on the person is abrogated.[32]

Articles 293 and 294, and the legislative commentaries surrounding their enactment, seem to leave no room for the private space envisaged by modern defenders of the practice of euthanasia. While noting that assisting in a "serious request for suicide" is different from murder, the language still clearly indicates that it is a criminal act. It is to be prohibited not because it is an attack "against the life of a particular person," but rather because it violates "respect . . . due human life in general." Thus, while granting the possibility of extreme circumstances that might lead individuals to consider and engage in assistance with suicide, the statutes place greater importance on the more general principle of societal respect for life.

If the reasoning here seems unusual—at least to an English-speaking audience—it may derive in part from the differences in legal heritage between the Anglo-Saxon legal tradition and the Roman legal tradition, under which the Netherlands operates.[33] Again, a thorough analysis is beyond the scope of this study, but several important distinctions emerge that are critical to an understanding of the Dutch position on euthanasia.[34]

First, the Dutch do not use juries in adjudicating legal matters; judges or panels of judges (appointed for life) render all decisions. Second, although there is a tradition of case law and legal precedent, a stronger tradition in Dutch jurisprudence compels judges to follow statutory law. Thus, although judges may cite previous cases in their decisions, they must technically interpret the findings of cases based on what has been formally codified as law. To do otherwise places the judgments in jeopardy of being overturned or enjoined, *pro forma,* by a higher court.

Finally, and perhaps most importantly, the tradition under which Dutch law operates places a heavier emphasis on the commonweal— the larger public good—than on individual rights:

People have rights here, but that is not usually the way a case is argued. The conflict of rights is just a piece of a larger area. How does it conform to established codes? Where does the boundary between the private and the public exist? If it can be shown there is no public detriment, the tradition is for the law to be silent . . . but if there is public harm, then that is a more important point than private rights.[35]

The responsibility for adjudicating cases based on the common good falls not only to judges but also initially to the *procureurs,* the prosecuting attorneys in each district, and to the *procureurs-general,* the attorneys general who supervise the enforcement of the laws in the Netherlands. Sutorius amplifies the notion of prosecutorial prerogatives thus:

At the most basic level—at the level of whether or not to prosecute a case—we give much power to our prosecutors. They not only make determination of whether grounds exist for suspicion of criminality, but whether such activity would serve the public interest in going to trial. He must investigate . . . but does not need to prosecute.[36]

This discretionary power given to the district attorneys finds expression, for example, in the decision to dismiss or prosecute a case of euthanasia. Prosecutors are bound to investigate any case that comes to their attention that is publicly a case of euthanasia (when "euthanasia" is listed on a death certificate, for example), or where (less frequently) someone accuses a physician who practices euthanasia of committing homicide. However, district attorneys are not bound to prosecute, even if there has been a formal violation of Article 293 of the Penal Code.

The prosecutors investigating a case take guidance from statutory law but also rely on precedent and the guidelines established by each precedent. "So," says Sutorius, "when someone says Roman law is statutory, the picture is not complete." Some acts that are statutorily illegal, such as euthanasia, never reach litigation:

This is where more informal rules work. Yes, there has been a violation—a person was killed—but the prosecutor asks other questions too. Was the person who killed a doctor? Did the patient request it? Were there good reasons for the request? Sometimes, these questions can be answered very quickly, positively, or negatively. If positively, then the matter often ends there. If negatively, then there should be an autopsy . . . what you would say an "inquest" . . . and more questions. If the answer is still negative, then there is a trial.[37]

Even if there is a trial, Sutorius and others have pointed out that exceptions may still be made to Article 293.[38] Judges in the Netherlands, though bound by statutory law, have been increasingly reluctant to punish physicians who practice euthanasia within certain guidelines.

The development of these guidelines, however, has followed a rather serpentine path. Permission to perform euthanasia, for example, has never been expressly given by the courts. Rather, the courts have indicated instances in which they would likely forgive, suspend, or dismiss outright a conviction under Article 293. Thus, what pass for guidelines are conditions that, if met, mitigate and temper the court's judgment on the physician's activities. When the Dutch speak of the "legal status" of euthanasia, then, they are referring to a body of judicial opinions, some of which are expansive in their view of permissible euthanasia, others of which are more restrictive, and some of which flatly contradict each other.[39] (See Table 1 for a summary of these court cases.) Seven opinions issued by various Dutch courts between 1973 and 1986 merit special attention. (See Table 1 for a summary of these court cases.)

Leeuwarden, 1973

The first set of guidelines that addressed the euthanasia issue came out of an opinion of the lower court in Leeuwarden in 1973. The case involved a doctor charged under Article 293 for killing her mother, a resident of a nursing home, at the mother's request. The facts of the case—which went uncontested by the defendant—can be briefly summarized:

1. The mother, 78 years old, had been a resident of an unnamed nursing home from September 1971 until she was euthanized in October of that same year.
2. Although the mother's underlying pathology is not specified, we know from the case records that she was wheelchair-bound, incontinent, and partially deaf; we may also surmise that she was clinically depressed and suffering the aftermath of a cerebrovascular accident of undetermined severity.
3. The mother had recently recovered from a bout of pneumonia and, during the acute phase of that illness, had fallen out of bed several times.[40]
4. The head nurse at the nursing home testified that while ill with pneumonia, the mother had said to him several times: "Isn't there anything to kill me, I want to die, I just want to die."

TABLE 1 Selected Court Rulings on Euthanasia in the Netherlands

Year	Court	Ruling and Significance
1973	District (Leeuwarden)	Convicted physician under Article 293; suspended sentence.
1977	Disciplinary (Amsterdam)	Acquitted physician for giving patient barbiturate overdose.
1981	District (Rotterdam)	Convicted nonphysician of assisting in suicide; established guidelines under which euthanasia is excused.
1982	District (Alkmaar)	Acquitted physician for practicing euthanasia; principle of "self-determination" as grounds for acquittal; judgment appealed by prosecutor.
1983	Appeals (Amsterdam)	Convicted physician from Alkmaar case on appeal; did not impose sentence; physician appealed.
1984	Supreme Court (the Hague)	Reversed Amsterdam Court of Appeals as restrictive and for not considering question of "conflict of duties"; referred case to the Hague Court of Appeals with instructions to broaden scope of question.
1986	Appeals (the Hague)	Acquitted physician under guidelines established by the Supreme Court.

SOURCES: Roose, interview with author; Henk Rigter, Els Borst-Eilers, and H. J. J. Leenen, "Euthanasia Across the North Sea," *British Medical Journal* 297 (17 December 1988): 1593–959; Eugene Sutorius, "A Mild Death for Paragraph 293 of the Netherlands Criminal Code?" (photocopy of a summary statement, Arnhem, 1985), 5–8; H. J. J. Leenen, "Euthanasia, Assistance to Suicide, and the Law: Developments in the Netherlands," *Health Policy* 8 (1987): 200–202; Admiraal, interview with author.

5. Moreover, the head nurse also characterized the mother as a "difficult patient to rehabilitate and to activate because she did not cooperate and obviously lacked the will to live."[41]

6. Finally, on October 19, the defendant injected her mother with 200 milligrams of morphine, with the intent of ending her mother's life. In fact, the mother expired within several minutes of administration of the morphine.[42]

The court in this case prefaced its opinions with the expert testimony of a medical inspector in the district.[43] Because the court's pro-

nouncement leans heavily on his testimony, it is worth quoting at
length:

> According to the expert witness, a doctor and medical inspector of na-
> tional health, the average physician in the Netherlands no longer con-
> siders it right that the life of a patient be stretched to the bitter end
> when the following conditions are present:
>
> A. [When] it concerns a patient who is incurable because of illness or
> accident—which may or may not be coupled with shorter or longer pe-
> riods of improvement or decline—or who must be regarded as incura-
> bly ill from a medical standpoint.
> B. Subjectively, his physical or spiritual suffering is unbearable and
> serious to the patient.
> C. The patient has indicated in writing, it could even be beforehand,
> that he desires to terminate his life, in any case that he wants to be de-
> livered from his suffering.
> D. According to medical opinion, the dying phase has begun for the
> patient or is indicated.
> E. Action is taken by the doctor, that is, the attending physician or
> medical specialist, or in consultation with that physician.
>
> [When all of the above conditions are present] it is widely accepted
> in medical circles in our country and also by the expert witness, that in
> order to relieve the suffering of the patient completely, or as much as
> possible, ever larger doses of medicine are administered . . . and that
> the administering physician then is fully aware and accepts that the
> good intended, namely the alleviation of suffering, brings with it the
> shortening of the patient's life.[44]

The court decline to accept condition D above,[45] but it took the other
opinions of the medical expert as generally established and acceptable
medical practice.

Based on this understanding of the state of medical affairs and on
the undisputed facts of the case, the court found fault with the defendant because her actions did not aim at alleviation of her mother's suffering but at directly killing her mother. The defendant's claim that
her mother's situation left her no alternative was explicitly rejected by
the court: "The appeal to a situation beyond one's control in the sense
of a (psychical) dire distress is not valid . . . [because] the accused . . .
did not take the course of alleviation indicated above . . . instead administering a lethal dose all at one time.[46] However, having established the doctor's intent and the method pursued as fact—and both
being sufficient to establish criminality—the court found itself unable

to pass the statutory sentence. Instead, in consideration of the "circumstances under which it was perpetrated . . . and the perfect purity of [the defendant's] motives beyond doubt," the court held in abeyance (for one year) a prison sentence of one week. If at the end of the year the doctor were found guilty of no other punishable act, the sentence would be completely suspended.[47]

That this case should stand as a landmark in the legal evolution of permissible euthanasia in the Netherlands is surprising on several counts. The facts of the case point to a poorly disguised case of medical killing.[48] The mother had been in the nursing home less than two months. She was recovering from an acute illness (pneumonia) superimposed on a more serious, debilitating lesion (a cerebrovascular accident, or stroke). Nevertheless, there was no indication in the records that her condition was lethal, nor that her case was "terminal" under even the most liberal definitions of the term. She exhibited classic signs of clinical depression, yet she was not started on a regimen of antidepressant therapy. Moreover, the request to die came in the midst of this ambiguous clinical setting, casting at least some doubt on the stability of the request. Finally, the agent in this case, the daughter, though a physician, was not an employee of the nursing home, nor was she responsible (in a professional sense) for her mother's medical care.

Given these facts, the court's conviction and sentencing of the defendant were largely symbolic. What the court seemed to say was that though there were formal grounds for conviction here, it found sufficient absence of malice for justice (in their eyes) to demand something milder.[49] Thus, while the court did not expressly sanction euthanasia, the fact that it failed to punish so undisguised an act of euthanasia seemed to suggest the possibility of legal tolerance of the activity.

The Leeuwarden court's decision opened, but did not settle, the legal boundaries within which euthanasia could be practiced. The inclusion of the phrase "purity of motives," the symbolic penalty handed down, and the court's silence on other irregularities of the case, gave impetus to what seemed to be a growing sentiment among the Dutch that euthanasia was acceptable under some circumstances.[50]

Leenen's gloss on this case is less tentative than my own. He finds an explicit acceptance of euthanasia in the court's opinion and further suggests that the guidelines quoted above refer specifically to acts of euthanasia:

> In the [Leeuwarden] decision the court stated that euthanasia would have been acceptable if: the patient is incurably ill; the patient suffers

unbearably; the patient has requested the termination of his life; [and] the termination of the patient's life is performed by the doctor who treats the patient or in concert with him.[51]

Although most of Leenen's colleagues have agreed with him, it is difficult to find that precise language in the court's opinion. In fact, had the court's decision been as explicit as Leenen suggests, the legal standing of euthanasia might have been less tenuous and might have been settled earlier than was otherwise the case.[52]

Rotterdam, 1981

There was a lag of eight years after the Leeuwarden decision before a district court ruled again on the legal status of euthanasia.[53] In 1981, the district court in Rotterdam convicted a layperson of assisting in a suicide. In passing sentence, the court keyed in on the fact that the defendant was not a physician. In its explanatory note, however, the Rotterdam court was bolder and more specific than the Leeuwarden court in outlining instances under which an act of euthanasia might escape legal sanction. The Rotterdam court lists nine criteria that, at a minimum, must be met if an act of euthanasia is to be excused:

1. There must be unbearable suffering on the part of the patient.
2. The desire to die must emanate from a conscious person.
3. The request for euthanasia must be voluntary.
4. The patient must have been given alternatives and must have had time to consider them.
5. There must be no other reasonable solutions to the patient's problem.
6. The death does not inflict unnecessary suffering on others.
7. More than one person must be involved in the decision.
8. Only a physician may actually euthanize the patient.
9. Great care must be exercised in making this decision.[54]

The opinion of the Rotterdam court signaled a decisive turn in the legal fortunes of euthanasia in the Netherlands. Where the Leeuwarden court was discreet and tentative, the Rotterdam court addressed itself directly to the matter of euthanasia and explicitly stated that the guidelines it enunciated applied unambiguously to active euthanasia (and not, for example, to the "distorted silhouettes of euthanasia" that Leenen mentions).

It is important to note, however, that although the Rotterdam decision created new categories in its guidelines and amplified on others, the language of the decision itself is remarkably flexible. It says, for example, that there must be "unbearable suffering" on the patient's part, and that the request must come from a "conscious person." Moreover, the court stipulates that the request must be voluntary. The court is silent, however, on how one ascertains "unbearable suffering" or the voluntariness of a request.[55] Moreover, the court did not say how the physician was to document these characteristics of a patient's condition. The court also suggests that euthanasia is a recourse of last resort. The patient has to be given "alternatives," for example, and euthanasia may be given when there are no "reasonable solutions" to the patient's condition (again, without giving a precise definition of what is meant by reasonableness or alternatives).

Finally, the court's decision ends with three safeguards for the practice. The first two are procedural: the decision to perform euthanasia must be collaborative, and only a physician may perform euthanasia. Although these two stipulations respond directly to the specifics of the particular case the court was deciding (a nonphysician had assisted in a suicide with no documented outside consultation), the court found them sufficiently prudent to include in its general guidelines.[56] The court's final pronouncement—that "great care be exercised"—was less of a guideline than an instruction to the medical profession to decide how to delineate what constitutes careful practice: "They [the courts] told us [the medical profession] we had to be responsible, and to decide what it means to be responsible in this area."[57]

The decision of the Rotterdam court, with its broad guidelines and its tacit endorsement of euthanasia as an acceptable medical practice, created great public debate. Most comments on the decision—both lay and professional—were favorable.[58] Following publication of this decision, however, the Ministry of Justice felt compelled to respond with some regulatory mechanism. The court's decision was sufficiently vague that the government decided that—at the very least—it needed to provide further elaboration on the public limits of this practice.[59] How, for example, were the court's guidelines to be realized in practice? The solution implemented by the minister of justice was to insist that every case of euthanasia brought to a prosecutor's attention be discussed at the regular meetings of the heads of the prosecution at the courts of appeals.[60] At these meetings, the decision to prosecute or not would be decided by consensus among the district attorneys present, and their deliberations would be guided by the criteria elaborated by the Leeuwarden and Rotterdam courts. As one lawyer notes:

> It was an imperfect decision, but the minister of justice had to provide some structure [to the prosecutors' decision]. Remember, this was a new practice in the public, and there could be much variation in prosecution. The meetings gave some uniform shape to the decisions, but left room for the private judgement of those involved. . . . Everyone had to follow the Rotterdam court—that was the rule—but not everyone was going to make the same interpretation.[61]

This "imperfect" arrangement among the courts, the government, and the medical profession, provided some shape to the boundaries of the practice, but it by no means settled the issue. Physicians had been given one signal that the practice of euthanasia would not be strictly interpreted under Article 293 of the Penal Code (at least not by the Rotterdam court), but they were given no assurance that they would not be prosecuted. Moreover, once they were prosecuted, there was no statutory assurance that another court would not choose to ignore the Rotterdam decision. Given a zealous prosecutor and a judge with a penchant for the literal wording of the law, a physician practicing euthanasia could still be charged and convicted of a felony.

Alkmaar, 1982

It was precisely this ambiguity and variation that came into play in an extremely important case that eventually made its way to the Supreme Court of the Netherlands. In 1982, a physician in Purmerend was prosecuted for terminating the life of an elderly patient at the patient's request. The district court in Alkmaar accepted the following findings in the case:

1. The patient was a 95-year-old woman, frail and in deteriorating health (the court record does not specify an illness), with no reasonable prospect for improvement.[62]
2. The patient "suffered severely" from her condition. She had "a clear mind and an independent spirit," and she considered dependance on another person as intolerable.[63]
3. She had repeatedly requested her physician to end her life.
4. One week before her death, she became acutely ill, lost consciousness, and on awakening found herself unable to speak or take nourishment by mouth.
5. A few days later, she was able to speak, eat, and drink again,

and this time she insisted to her physician that she could not go through another similar experience.

6. The physician consulted with another doctor about the case and decided to accede to the patient's request. He gave her "two injections" (the contents of which are unspecified), and the patient expired.[64]

The Alkmaar court acquitted the physician, basing its decision on two principles. It decided, first, that the patient had a right to self-determination and that her request to be killed fell broadly within the scope of this principle of autonomy. It further established that the physician had carefully determined the seriousness of the request and that the request was well documented. The act, according to the court, was thus essentially not wrongful, and the physician was not guilty of "material illegality."[65] In other words, no crime had been committed.

The prosecutor in this case decided to appeal the court's decision.[66] It seemed to the prosecutor that the Alkmaar court had not given sufficient weight to the guidelines laid down by the previous Rotterdam decision and had, moreover, ignored other details of the case. Specifically, the assertion that there was an absence of "material illegality" struck the prosecutor as an instance of a district court making up law out of whole cloth.[67]

Amsterdam, 1983

The Amsterdam Court of Appeals, to which the prosecutor's petition went, agreed to retry the case and subsequently found the physician guilty under Article 293 (but assigned no punishment). The Amsterdam court not only agreed with the prosecution's contention that there was "material illegality" (the law clearly had been violated) but also implicitly criticized earlier court rulings on the matter. The argument that euthanasia had achieved sufficient consensus and definition to be acceptable

> fails because when one takes into account that this complicated question is being studied by a State Commission [and when one sees] the evident dangers connected with euthanasia, one cannot speak of a present adequately crystallized general view on the basis of which euthanasia . . . can be regarded as generally and socially acceptable.[68]

The appeals court also implicitly rejected the lower court's finding of "unbearable suffering" on the patient's part and doubted that her doctor "had no other choice than to spare her that suffering through euthanasia."[69]

In summary, then, the Amsterdam court's conviction of the physician rested on two findings that differed with the lower court: the practice of euthanasia was still "materially illegal" inasmuch as Article 293 was still law, and the physician failed to justify an exception to the rule in this case because he could not demonstrate that the patient's suffering left him no reasonable alternative.

The Supreme Court, 1984

The physician in the Amsterdam case, in turn, appealed the court's decision (this time with the assistance of the Netherlands Society for Voluntary Euthanasia [*Nederlands Vereniging voor Vrijwillige Euthanasie,* or NVVE]) to the Supreme Court of the Netherlands.[70] The Supreme Court's ruling, handed down in November 1984, was complicated and tentative and was widely criticized.[71] The high court agreed with the prosecution that there was "material illegality"—Article 293 had been violated by the physician in question. Moreover, the earlier exception defined by the Alkmaar court (that the doctor was helping the patient exercise her right to self-determination) was also explicitly rejected by the high court.[72] In this sense, the complete victory that the physician and his supporters in the NVVE had hope for failed to materialize.

On the other hand, the high court strongly criticized the Amsterdam court for not having raised *other* questions and for not having considered *other* aspects of the case that might have been more appropriate grounds for exempting the doctor's actions from punishment. Were there truly other ways of alleviating the patient's suffering (as the Amsterdam court had suggested), and if so, what were they? The Amsterdam court had been silent on this point. More important, the Supreme Court said that the lower court had failed to consider whether the physician himself was placed in an intolerable position because of what it called a "conflict of duties."[73] Was the patient's suffering such that the physician was forced to act in a situation "beyond [his] control"?[74] The Supreme Court overturned the lower court's verdict because the latter had decided the matter from too limited a perspective, and it referred the case to the Court of Appeals of the Hague. In referring the case, the Supreme Court instructed the Hague court to consider the above questions in light of what it considered one overarching consideration: "Whether the euthanasia practiced by the accused would, *from an objective medical perspective,* be regarded as an action justified in a situation of necessity (beyond one's control.)"[75] In other words, had medical practice sufficiently changed so that a contemporary physician could reasonably claim that some exceptional situations demanded euthanasia?

The Hague, 1986

The phrasing of the Supreme Court's instructions left the appeals court in the Hague in an unenviable position. The Supreme Court had stated that because of the "evident dangers connected with euthanasia" there was, as yet, no "adequately crystallized general view" on the acceptability of euthanasia. And yet, the Supreme Court's instructions demanded that the lower court decide the issue from "an objective medical perspective." However, as critics of the Supreme Court's decision noted, physicians are no less members of society than anyone else; if there was no general, societal consensus on the permissibility of euthanasia (as the court suggested), then the same should be assumed for the medical profession. To suggest that the medical profession, *en masse,* had some peculiarly revelatory insight into the matter (which it had not yet shared with the public) betrayed an alarming ingenuousness about the profession's uniformity; alternatively, it expressed a cry of distress from the court for some authoritative, extra-legal guidance on the matter.[76]

Nevertheless, bound by the higher court's order, the prosecutor at the Hague requested that the KNMG give its opinion on the acceptability of euthanasia from the profession's standpoint. Specifically, the prosecutor asked this medical organization to consider the concept of "conflict of duties," which had figured prominently in the accused's earlier defense and which the Supreme Court had indicated was a critical question. The executive board of the organization responded with the following summary statement:

> [In] a decision to honor a request for euthanasia, the point of departure has always been that the doctor and the patient must stand with their backs to the wall, that is to say, that they no longer see any possibility of making the suffering of the patient bearable. [This point of departure in so far as manifests a resemblance to the judicial concept of a situation of necessity [*force majeure*], that proceeding on the basis of a number of medical ethical principles, a path is chosen which is the least unacceptable to both the doctor and the patient.] There is, in that instance, a conflict between the principle that the doctor on the one hand has the duty to do everything in his power to save life, and that a doctor on the other hand has the duty to find an answer to the explicit wish of

the patient who finds himself in a situation of necessity. The corollary is that a doctor will have to give serious weight to a justified request which meets the criteria posited in law and by the KNMG, and that honoring such a request can be justified. The doctor is thus confronted with a conflict of duties of such a nature, that one can indeed speak of a situation of necessity in the sense indicated by the High Court.[77]

The opinion of the KNMG was notable on a number of counts. The medical association stated that there were occasions in the practice of medicine that could be considered "situations of necessity," that is, situations in which either the patient or the physician (or both) found himself or herself under such duress that euthanasia might be justifiable. Thus, the KNMG essentially accepted the court's definition.

This point is not to be minimized. The concept of *force majeure,* or "situation of necessity," is essentially a legal term. It arises in response to a predicament: how is the law to treat one who has committed a crime but whose actions were the direct result of coercion or duress? The principle of jurisprudence that operates here, *force majeure,* does not pretend that there has been no transgression. Rather, it holds that the agent of the criminal act is partially or entirely blameless because of the circumstances under which the action occurred. The nature of the act—its basic *illegality*—does not change; what changes is the law's response. Persons charged with a crime who successfully argue that they acted under "a situation of necessity" may have their convictions suspended or the penalty for their crime waived or reduced.

In accepting the language of the high court, however, the KNMG essentially said that the same concept applies to medical practice. In other words, there may be situations in which a physician is forced by "necessity" to act in a manner contrary to law or, perhaps more precisely, in a manner that violates the very tenets of the profession. The reasoning of the court—and, by analogy, of the KNMG—followed a middle path: euthanasia was not to be sanctioned per se, but physicians who practiced euthanasia could escape punishment by showing that they acted under force majeure. Perhaps more tellingly, the KNMG also stated that there was a positive duty on the part of the physician to "find an answer" to a patient's request for euthanasia. Thus, the KNMG stated, if their own guidelines and the guidelines of the courts were followed, then euthanasia would be justified.

Basing its decision heavily on the opinion of the KNMG, the Hague court dismissed the charges against the physician. The court reasoned that there were "no norms of medical ethics that forbade his actions." Moreover, it also observed that many contemporary physicians in the Netherlands "consider active life termination as medically-ethically possible."[78] Based on these considerations, the physician's deliberate care, and the well-documented wishes of the patient, the court found no grounds for conviction.

This last case helped to crystallize what now seems to be a norm of practice in cases of euthanasia. The court gave heavy emphasis to the patient's right to self-determination (an appeal that earlier courts had found insufficient to merit exception to Article 293). The court also established that though there was still disagreement, the medical profession in the Netherlands did not necessarily consider an act of euthanasia, per se, to be unacceptable medical practice. Under some circumstances, in fact, the KNMG had suggested that it was a physician's duty to act.[79] Perhaps most importantly, the lower court rejected the stronger language of the Supreme Court, which had asked for "objective medical criteria." The Appeals Court of the Hague substituted the phrase "*reasonable* medical insight."[80] Thus, absent a uniform standard on what constitutes a "situation of necessity," the court referred the matter to medical *opinion* (as opposed to some standardized protocol, for example).

Two other points in the court's decision are noteworthy. The patient in this case was not terminal, nor was she in acute physical pain. The court ruled, nevertheless, that "psychic suffering" or the "potential disfigurement of personality" could be acceptable grounds for requesting euthanasia. Thus, while not granting the validity of all requests for euthanasia, the court did expand the circle of claims. Secondly, the court's ruling also leaned heavily on the particular judgment of the individual physician: it was the physician, in agreement with the patient, who determined that the patient's circumstances merited euthanasia.[81]

THE PROFESSIONAL RESPONSE TO EUTHANASIA

By the end of 1986, there was enough judicial precedent in the Netherlands to suggest that under certain circumstances, physicians practicing euthanasia would probably not be prosecuted, and if prosecuted, they would be treated leniently. This situation, however, was less than satisfying to a number of groups in Dutch society, especially physicians:

It would have been better simply to have drafted a law. We can make such a law now. But as the [situation now exists], there is messiness everywhere. Doctors aren't sure what the guidelines mean—we are doctors, after all, not lawyers—and there are many unfriendly people to this practice who can create mischief . . . call the police for example. Also, you always technically have to involve the prosecutor in these cases. . . . Article 293 stands . . . and that takes time, it embarrasses the family who should be taking time to grieve.[82]

Because of this "messiness," the current situation was also a problem for public prosecutors: many (and probably most) physicians who practice euthanasia misstate the cause of death on death certificates. Thus, prosecutors, who occupy the frontline in enforcement of the laws, find themselves unable to regulate a practice that, by default, has come under their supervision.

In 1984, before the Hague decision came down, the KNMG had sent a letter to the minister of justice, asking for a change in the laws to permit euthanasia. The KNMG's request created a stir, especially among a group of more traditional physicians, many of whom resigned from the organization in protest.[83] The Council of State deferred the matter because, it said, there was already substantial litigation in this area, it would be prudent to await the judicial decision; most importantly, its own State Commission on Euthanasia had not yet issued its report.[84]

In the interim, however, the KNMG issued its own set of guidelines.[85] The KNMG notes at the outset that it does not intend to discuss the ethical principles governing the practice of euthanasia. The guidelines, it says, are intended "as a practical guide."[86] The KNMG statement accepts at the outset the established definition of the practice: "Euthanasia is understood [as] an action which aims at taking the life of another at the latter's expressed request. It concerns an action of which death is the purpose and the result."[87] The preamble to the statement further distinguishes euthanasia from "euthanasia-like" actions that would not fall into this definition, such as cessation of unwanted or futile treatment. Further, the organization notes that euthanasia, "is and remains an *ultimum refugium* (a last resort)" and should be considered only in exceptional or extreme cases.[88] Lastly, the preamble stipulates that the responsibility for euthanasia remains with the physician (not the nurse), and that only physicians themselves may perform euthanasia.[89]

The guidelines list five general criteria that—at a minimum—a physician must meet in giving euthanasia: (1) voluntariness on the patient's part; (2) a well considered request; (3) stability of desire; (4) unacceptable suffering; and (5) collegial consultation. These criteria, though they receive further elaboration in the document, leave a good deal open to professional judgment, and the KNMG notes elsewhere that the guidelines assume the good intentions and professional competence of practitioners.[90]

The first three criteria deal with the question of the patient's free will and powers of discernment. The stipulation that a request be voluntary addresses the fear that a patient's expression of a desire to die may be the result of coercion and might reflect, for example, an overburdened caregiver's fatigue rather than the patient's true wishes. Alternatively, the KNMG elsewhere notes that some requests for euthanasia derive from other factors: a fear of pain, loneliness, a sense that one has become superfluous or burdensome to family and friends.[91] An initial request for euthanasia, the guidelines suggest, should be examined carefully, and if alternative solutions can be found to the problems that gave rise to the patient's request, they should be attempted first.

The next two stipulations—that the request be well considered and that the desire be stable—address the more subtle problem of a patient's competence to make this decision.[92] Thus, the request to die has to be an expression of an enduring desire: impulsive decisions arising from temporary circumstances, for example, or decisions made in the midst of a depression should not be approved.[93] The KNMG statement encourages physicians practicing euthanasia to document the patient's persistent requests. Although the guidelines set no minimum number of requests before euthanasia is considered a "stable desire," it does say that one request alone will not suffice. Finally, the statement says at the outset that the guidelines apply only to patients who are cognitively intact and who are capable of making such a request.[94]

The last two criteria address the questions of professional judgment and professional responsibility. The phrase "unacceptable suffering" is not precisely defined, nor is it restricted to physical suffering. Nevertheless, KNMG notes that although the interpretation of suffering is necessarily subjective, it expects that

> the doctor, taking into account the personality, intelligence, life's history, and the life and world view of the patient, and what he can understand on the basis of his insight as a doctor gained from intensive and

repeated conversations with the patient, should reasonably be able to come to a judgement that the suffering of the patient must be viewed as unbearable.[95]

The guidelines go on to point out that recent jurisprudence on the matter had given great weight to the patient's dignity and whether additional suffering would "tarnish the patient's personality."[96] The KNMG, taking note of the courts' opinions, suggests in its guidelines that the physician, in considering whether or not to perform euthanasia, needs to be concerned with the potential loss of the patient's dignity that additional suffering might entail. The wording of the guidelines, moreover, suggests that absent objective standards on what constitutes unbearable suffering, the responsibility for this determination falls to the physician.

The last criterion of the guidelines insists that the physician in question consult with at least one other colleague and also suggests that clerics, psychologists, and others may also be queried. It is not specified, however, whether the consultation should be with an objective third party (who would, presumably, be more disinterested and who could act as a brake on a poorly reasoned decision). In fact, the commentary on this guideline suggests that a suitable person for consultation might be another physician who had been directly involved in the patient's care. Moreover, the KNMG seems more concerned with questions of confidentiality than with objectivity here. It suggests to physicians that they limit the number of people involved in consultation so as not to compromise the patient's right to privacy.[97]

The statement on guidelines ends with a short section called "Euthanasia in Practice." This addendum moves from the more general criteria described above to the mechanics of honoring a request for euthanasia. This section, however, is only slightly more specific than the five principles on which it elaborates. It notes, for example, that the request for euthanasia often comes when family members are present and that only the patient may make a valid request (suggesting, without specifying how, that the physician must ascertain that the patient is not being coerced). It further reiterates that only a doctor may accede to the request and adds a clause exempting conscientious objectors from participating in the procedure.

This final clause deserves closer scrutiny. The KNMG understands that some doctors, for whatever reasons, cannot bring themselves to practice euthanasia. These physicians may excuse themselves from such cases, but they cannot be further involved in the decision-making process "because there can be no question of an objective participation in the decision for euthanasia."[98] Moreover, a doctor declining to euthanize for religious or moral reasons (as opposed to strictly medical criteria) is bound to refer the patient to another physician who feels no such scruples. This section concludes with the hope that physicians and their patients will have discussed their respective positions on euthanasia at the "earliest possible stage so that they are not confronted with [unexpected] surprises at a moment when discussion is already difficult."[99]

It should be noted that the guidelines are silent on two points. They give no instructions about the method to be employed in performing euthanasia, and they make no note of how the physician is to enter the patient's demise on the death certificate (though they suggest that the public prosecutor be notified). This latter point is particularly important and demonstrates a tension between the KNMG's guidelines and the legal standing of euthanasia.[100] The KNMG notes in its final paragraph that though the courts in the Netherlands show leniency in this matter, euthanasia remains punishable by law. It further states that the public prosecutor will initiate an investigation if the doctor does *not* enter a declaration of natural death, but the KNMG does not instruct its physicians on the appropriate wording in the death certificate. In fact, the wording of the guidelines suggests that physicians might responsibly obscure the exact cause of death because "they—unlike other citizens—are not obligated to report a crime against life."[101] Moreover, the KNMG notes that medical personnel are entitled to professional secrecy and, further, suggests that physicians may claim that privilege before a judge.[102]

Irrespective of these latter two omissions, the guidelines issued by the KNMG seem a fair response to the challenge implicitly posed to it by the courts. If euthanasia were to be permitted, and if Article 293 remained unchanged, the courts seemed to say, there needed to be some criteria by which to define permissibility. Clearly, the courts wanted to restrict euthanasia to medical practice, but just as clearly, they found no established consensus within the profession on euthanasia. The KNMG's response, in turn, was to issue guidelines under which euthanasia *might* be acceptable medical practice (the KNMG did not formally endorse the practice of euthanasia).[103] If the criteria seemed vague, they in part reflected the vague instructions of the courts. Since there was no widely held position within the medical profession on the permissibility of euthanasia, an appeal to "*objective medical criteria*" (to use the Supreme Court's language) was bound to result in an incomplete answer. The best that the KNMG could do was to paint with broadest strokes the boundaries within which the practice might gain acceptance.

THE POLITICAL RESPONSE TO EUTHANASIA

The KNMG's equivocal statement also reflected the unsettled political atmosphere surrounding this question. Since 1973, the NVVE and others had been working to liberalize the restrictions on euthanasia that were based on Article 293, but with little success. Although the association had garnered public support (including thirty thousand active members as of the end of 1988), it had been unable to effect a change in the laws.[104] However, the Rotterdam decision of 1981, with its tacit acceptance of euthanasia under some circumstances, created a stir in governmental circles because of what was seen as an "exercise in creative jurisprudence."[105] In 1982, at the urging of her minister of justice, Queen Beatrix created the State Commission on Euthanasia and charged its members with the task of recommending possible legislative reforms on euthanasia and assisted suicide.[106]

Before the commission could issue its findings and recommendations, however, a member of the D'66 party in the lower house of Parliament entered a bill independently that would have formally legalized euthanasia practiced by physicians. The Wessel-Tuinstra bill (so named after the member of parliament who introduced it) would have amended the Penal Code so as to abrogate in part the restrictions of Article 293. It was an attempt to legalize—not decriminalize—euthanasia so that "it would not be punishable in the framework of careful rendering of assistance to a person who is in a hopeless situation."[107] Although the bill became the focal point of sharp debate both inside and outside the government, Parliament took no action pending the report of the state commission.[108]

The report of the state commission, which it finally released on 19 August 1985, was an involved document, divided into three parts.[109] The relevant section of the document contained the recommendations to the queen for legislative reform on the practice of euthanasia.[110] The commission's recommendations supported or incorporated many of the earlier judicial and professional pronouncements on euthanasia, including the definition of euthanasia as the active, intentional termination of life.[111] The majority of the commission members, moreover, agreed with the high court and with statements from the

KNMG that there were situations under which euthanasia would be permissible and suggested restrictions almost identical to those proposed in earlier judicial and professional statements.[112]

The commission members, however, were unable to agree on what circumstances surrounding a patient's condition would justify a request for euthanasia. Nine members (out of the fifteen who sat on the commission) used the phrase *in extremis* to describe a necessary condition for permissible euthanasia. In other words, the patient's suffering had to constitute an exceptional, rare circumstance, one in which there was no other medical alternative.[113] Four members, however, wanted the phrase amended further to include a more restrictive qualifier: "and whose impending death is inevitable." This additional language, some members felt, was needed to further define what they felt was too expansive a criterion. The notion of a "hopeless emergency situation" (which is how one of the majority members translated *in extremis*) could easily apply to a whole range of patients whose deaths were not imminent, and the minority group felt that—at least as an initial step—the language of a commission needed to be as constrained as possible.[114] Two members of the commission dissented from the commission's recommendations altogether and issued a separate minority report in which they urged the queen to disregard the commission's reforms, warning that the Netherlands would be making "a historic mistake" by removing prohibitions against euthanasia.[115]

Part of the objection contained in the minority report derived not only from the main recommendations of the commission, but from a more controversial passage that received little attention outside of the Netherlands. Although the commission had specifically stated at the outset of its report that euthanasia was to be countenanced only for conscious patients who could voluntarily give consent, a majority of the commission members (in fact, all but the two who dissented altogether) also suggested that for some patients in a persistent vegetative state, for whom "on the basis of objective medical scientific criteria no improvement may be expected," there might be justification for euthanasia.[116] Some who were generally inclined to support legal reforms to allow voluntary euthanasia were dismayed by the latter provision:

> They were really two separate questions. One is a matter of free will, the other is a more difficult question, how do you act, medically speaking, for people who cannot act for themselves? The commission, though, anticipated the later debate, perhaps too quickly. It might have been better not to have included this last problem [at the same time].[117]

Others have commented that this provision for comatose patients "created a lot of rumor," and created an internal inconsistency in the commission's own logic.[118] Still others, however, considered the extension of euthanasia to this latter category of patients an inevitable (and humane) next step.[119]

The actual legislative reform that the commission recommended, however, included provisions for amending Article 293 only to include exceptions concerning requests for euthanasia from conscious, competent patients. Acting on the commission's recommendation and on behalf of the government, the minister of justice and the minister of well-being, public health, and culture sent a letter to the Speaker of the lower house of Parliament with the outline of a model bill.[120] The government's recommendation (formally entered as a "trial bill" [*Proeve van een voorstel van wet met toelichting*]), was met with a counterproposal, again submitted by Wessel-Tuinstra of the D'66 party, who had reworked her earlier bill to conform more closely to the language of the commission's recommendations. The government bill, among other stipulations, would have restricted euthanasia to patients in whom there was a "concrete expectation of death," that is, patients who were considered terminal. The Wessel-Tuinstra bill, on the other hand, contained no such qualifier and proposed amending Article 293 to permit euthanasia for patients who were in "a hopeless situation."[121] Both bills contained "carefulness considerations" that reflected, in slightly different language, the criteria of the KNMG and the Hague Court of Appeals discussed above. The government bill, however, contained two additional provisions that represented, in part, attempts to appease particular members of the ruling coalition.[122] The "Note of Explication" attached to the bill expanded on the government's notion of a "concrete expectation of death" thus:

> That the expert [physician], according to prevailing medical insight, anticipates that the course of the disease will end in death, [and] therefore is incurable. The death of the patient concerned must then, according to medical insight, be inevitable in consequence of a death cause (sic) which cannot be eliminated nor stabilized.[123]

The note continues by suggesting that although it is impossible to define in law an "imminent" death more precisely than "weeks or days," it does stipulate that "the loss of vital organ functions [should have] already begun or is about to begin."[124] This stipulation, thus, would have effectively restricted euthanasia much more tightly than had previous court decisions and would certainly have narrowed considerably the scope of permissible euthanasia that had been outlined the year before by the KNMG.

At the same time, the government's proposal would have allowed euthanasia for unconscious patients who had previously documented this desire in the event of their incapacitation.[125] Similar in concept to "living will" legislation now so common in the United States, the ministerial proposal extended the notion to voluntariness so that competent patients who at some point envisaged situations in which they would be incapable of articulating their desires would be able prospectively to empower their physicians to administer euthanasia under specified conditions.[126] Although distinct from the commission's suggestion that performing euthanasia on permanently comatose patients might be permissible, the government's proposal did address itself to what it considered an unarticulated, but powerful, fear motivating some calls for liberalized euthanasia laws.[127]

Despite all of this legislative and judicial ferment and the government's specific endorsement of a reform bill, nothing by way of statutory reform on euthanasia has occurred in the Netherlands (at least through 1990). The bills submitted by the government and by Wessel-Tuinstra were both rejected by the Council of State, with the comment that "it would be preferable to await further jurisprudence from the High Council [Supreme Court] before the Lawgiver (Parliament) makes more definitive decisions."[128] What further jurisprudence the council expected at that point remains unclear. Both the Supreme Court and the Hague Court of Appeals had made distinct pleas in their decisions for professional and legislative guidance on the matter.

One observer suggests that the council was not awaiting further judicial guidance but simply waiting: "This is now a political question, not a judicial or ethical one. The government is a coalition [and has] many conservative members in it . . . a minority, no doubt, but enough to break the coalition. An example, I think, of democracy not being followed."[129] Another interpretation points to a second possibility: the council hesitates because it has a paucity of empirical evidence on the exact nature of the practice:

> The council is by tradition very cautious . . . and sees [changing the Penal Code] with suspicion. They perhaps want more knowledge, more actual knowledge, than we have. It is similar to what happened with abortion here: we had somewhat legal abortion for ten years, and

many proposals [for legalization], but no action. After a decade of
watching this practice, then we could pass laws. Something like this is
going to happen with euthanasia.[130]

Sutorius echoes this sentiment and notes with astonishment that little,
if any, empirical research has been done on the subject:

I once proposed—only with *some* humor—that we temporarily suspend [Article] 293, but force all doctors to write "euthanasia" [on the
death certificate] when it was euthanasia, then send a standard report
[for them to fill out]: age of patient, sex, disease, documentation, etc.
Then after two years, look at the practice, and decide how to change
293. Some people thought I was completely humorous, but really, this
idea is better than what we have right now.[131]

Sutorius's comment points to the obvious, but it is an element
often overlooked in this debate. Those in the Netherlands who want
formal protection for physicians who practice euthanasia suggest that
it is (and will remain) a rare occurrence. Those opposed suggest that
the practice is more widespread than suspected and that sanctioning
the practice will simply extend its reach to those not able to protect
themselves. Although both camps agree that euthanasia occurs with
some degree of regularity in the Netherlands, neither is able to give an
account that will pass careful scrutiny. What little is known is detailed
below and helps to explain, in part, the difficulty that governmental
institutions have had in trying to decide how to handle this matter of
euthanasia.

THE PREVALENCE OF EUTHANASIA

Without specifying precisely what they mean, the courts, government commissions, and professional health care organizations in the
Netherlands have generally suggested that euthanasia is an exceptional practice. It is not, for example, to be part of routine medical
care, nor is it to be considered the normal end even for a patient with
a lethal disease or in extreme pain or discomfort. The KNMG's phrase
"with their backs to the wall" is a vivid image used to describe what
they see as a permissible opening for euthanasia: it is to be practiced
only in a desperate situation.

The courts, though declining to accept the more emotionally

charged language of the KNMG, have also made it clear that if euthanasia is to be excused under the existing laws, the area beyond reach of the full force of Article 293 must be quite small indeed. It must be shown that the physician in question acted out of *force majeure*, a case in which the patient's suffering and cry for assistance with suicide were so compelling and, literally, so much "a greater force" that the physician, in observing his or her duty to attend to the patient's distress, was bound to break the law.

For the government, charged with enforcing the laws and opposed (at least officially) to eliminating or amending Article 293, the current status of euthanasia presents a serious challenge to its integrity and its ability to govern.[132] The district prosecutors, who must investigate all known cases of euthanasia, take guidance from the minister of justice. If the government orders investigations and prosecutions with too heavy a load, it could, potentially potentially, swamp the courts with euthanasia cases and disrupt the uneasy balance that currently exists. However, to ignore cases of euthanasia, or to leave them solely to the discretion and control of the medical profession, would in essence decriminalize an activity in which, the government has implicitly said, the state has a direct interest.[133] It has also been suggested that such an attitude could destroy the government's ruling coalition.[134]

This state of affairs considerably hampers answering another question on the public aspects of this practice, namely, how many people resort to euthanasia each year in the Netherlands? This question indirectly addresses the matter of the "exceptional" quality of this practice. What is meant by euthanasia's being rare, a tool of last recourse? What percentage of a country's mortality rate attributable to euthanasia would signal its excessive use or abuse, or alternatively, below what level would the government feel relatively secure that the practice was, in fact, exceptional?[135]

The answer to this question of prevalence receives an incomplete answer. The paucity of available information, moreover, is indicative of the peculiar fashion in which euthanasia has been tolerated. Thus, instead of a well-documented review of the available literature on this question, what I present here (by way of rounding out my discussion of the public state of euthanasia) is a compilation of what data and opinions are available. I further place these data in their context and evaluate to an extent the veracity we could reasonably attach to such figures (an exercise that has yet to appear in the literature).

It would have been desirable to have proceeded with this particular question using the government's health documents and statistics as a base. Even though the Dutch health care system is a mixture of public and private efforts (with a heavier emphasis on private financing), it maintains an extensive regulatory network that seems to assure a high degree of accessibility and quality to its citizens.[136] As a consequence, the Dutch central and provincial governments gather and analyze extensive records pertaining to the health of their people.

On the question of euthanasia, however, the government publishes no regular records. One obvious reason for this absence of data is that the government cannot, without great awkwardness, make an illicit practice part of its regular statistical survey of health practices.[137] For similar reasons, other national governmental and professional bodies that must, at least officially, remain neutral do not attempt to publish these data.[138] Moreover, the data from the Ministry of Justice, to which the legal regulation of this practice has fallen, is subject to the regularity with which the practice is either self-reported by physicians (by notifying the public prosecutor or by entering "euthanasia" on the death certificate) or reported by another party making an accusation. Despite the relatively liberalized interpretations of Article 293 handed down by the courts, physicians who do practice euthanasia tend not to report a case of euthanasia to the district prosecutors and are even less likely to enter "euthanasia" on the death certificate.[139]

Even if one can plausibly explain this lack of official governmental and professional record keeping, however, one is still struck by the paucity of empirical research on the subject by others. Given the importance of the question, the openness with which euthanasia is discussed in the media, and the number of physicians who have published statements of support for the practice in their professional journals, for example, it would have seemed a likely topic of inquiry for any number of universities or research groups during the past fifteen years.[140] And yet, by all accounts, this research has either not been done or has been inadequate. Dr. Helene Dupuis suggests that this is a topic that does not easily lend itself to empirical research:

> Really, if one agrees with [the possibility] of euthanasia, then what you are asking is for people to tell you about a most personal question: why do they want to die? If you do not believe euthanasia is a possibility, what more do you have to say? Any evidence here hits against a closed mind. But really, we do now have a lot of experience with euthanasia in this country . . . It is not formally [written up], but enough people can tell stories, or have seen this, that we know what it is.[141]

On the other hand, others are "baffled by the lack of knowledge," to quote Eugene Sutorius:

> Why has no one done this, I do not truly know. But maybe because it is an unhappy subject, or maybe we feel it is too private a problem. How many use euthanasia every year, no one can truly say. And if you ask if this does not make me, as a lawyer and once a prosecutor, uncomfortable, then of course it does, because we should know something more about what it is that people want, and how many times they want it.[142]

Still others, finally, have suggested that the tradition of empirical social research that has taken hold in the United States is not as strong in the Netherlands, nor does the Netherlands have what one observer called "this amazing quantity of universities" that exists in the United States.[143]

Thus, one is left to rely on what has been published and to evaluate not the prevalence of the practice but *other estimates* of the prevalence. The figures most frequently cited by discussants, and the sources for those figures, are listed in Table 2. One should note that the sources that do cite statistics on the practice, however, vary wildly in their estimate and are also of varying reliability.

The figure cited by the Ministry of Justice, to begin with the lowest estimate, is—by consensus—far too low. The figure this government department releases is simply a compilation of the number of cases of euthanasia investigated by its district attorneys in any given year, and is, thus, the only number of cases of euthanasia that the Dutch government officially recognizes to have occurred. The most recent data available encompassed the year 1987, and the government puts the cases of euthanasia at less than two hundred.[150]

The next estimate has to be deduced from the article by Rigter, Borst-Eilers and Leenen, cited above. The article, which was in response to a harsh assessment of the Dutch position on euthanasia by the Working Party on Euthanasia of the British Medical Association,[151] noted that "[euthanasia] would amount to only 2% of all deaths that occur in general practice in the Netherlands."[152] What precisely this means in terms of overall mortality is unclear.

The source given for this figure of 2% was a survey done in 1985, which sampled twenty-five practitioners, seventeen of whom had received requests for euthanasia and nine of whom had acceded to the request.[153] The article notes that if one extrapolated from this survey, the average general practitioner would perform euthanasia once every

TABLE 2   Estimates of the Prevalence of Euthanasia
in the Netherlands

Cases/Year	Source	Method
< 200	Ministry of Justice	Reports of prosecutors
3,000–3,600	Rigter, Borst-Eilers, and Leenen[144]	1985 survey of general practitioners[145]
< 5000	Admiraal[146]	Personal conclusion from 1987 survey of Amsterdam Department of Health[147]
5,000–10,000	Rigter[148]	1987 Amsterdam survey and unspecified sources
6,000–12,000	Dessaur and Rutenfrans[149]	Unspecified reports from "euthanasia advocates"

three years. There are approximately ten thousand general practitioners in the Netherlands.[154] Thus, one crude estimate of the
practice of euthanasia among general practitioners would be to take
one-third of the above number, resulting in approximately 3,300. Alternatively, if the Hague study is representative of the general population (and there are good reasons to doubt that it is), then twenty-five
doctors practicing euthanasia nine times would proportionally give
3,600 cases of euthanasia among ten thousand general practitioners
nationwide in a given year. One should note that, either way, Rigter's
numbers simply do not match published mortality statistics. If 3,300
cases of euthanasia represent 2% of the deaths in general practice in
the Netherlands in a given year, then the mortality rate solely in general practice (165,000) is higher than the published annual rate for the
country as a whole (120,000).[155]

Pieter Admiraal, perhaps the leading proponent of euthanasia in
the Netherlands among physicians, believes that this figure is too low
precisely because it does not account for deaths due to euthanasia that
occur outside the hands of general practitioners. He notes, for example, that in his experience a bare majority of people requesting euthanasia are terminal cancer patients, and as a rule, the majority of cancer patients in the Netherlands die in hospitals or specialty clinics (by
a ratio of 7 to 3). Thus, to the cases of euthanasia performed by gen-

eral practitioners, Admiraal would add "at least another 1,000" who died in institutions from euthanasia.[156]

Admiraal further notes that the surveys conducted in Amsterdam and in the Hague were probably not representative of the country as a whole: "Amsterdam and the coast towns are more liberal than the rest of the country. If you go to the south, where there are many Catholics, or north near the ocean, where many conservative Protestants live, you would probably not see such acceptance of euthanasia."[157] Nevertheless, Admiraal also suggests that the number of cases of euthanasia in institutions may be underrepresented. He notes, for example, that there are approximately 33,000 patients with terminal cancer every year in the Netherlands. Of these, he claims that approximately 15% receive euthanasia: "I don't have good data, but from talking to other doctors—from doctors who call for advice or talk to me in meetings— maybe 15% of cancer patients get euthanasia. So another number would be, perhaps, 4,000."[158] So, when pressed, Admiraal claims that the probable number of cases is less than 5,000.

Henk Rigter, who seems to have become the point person for the Health Council of the Netherlands on this issue, will suggest, in private, that a more appropriate estimate would be a range of from 5,000 to 10,000. In addition to the two surveys mentioned above (which, he admits, do not offer a particularly solid base from which to generalize), Rigter and his colleagues have the advantage of having sat on the hearings the Health Council conducted in 1987 to study possible reforms permitting euthanasia. He became convinced, he says, from the testimony of physicians and public health officials, that euthanasia is more widely accepted than was once thought, especially since the court decisions in 1981 and 1984. Although he is quick to point out that it is not the norm or a regular practice, he does suggest that for a portion of patients in distress, it has become an acceptable option and that there are more than enough doctors willing to accede to a request. Thus, he says, Admiraal's estimate of 5,000 is probably too low, but without saying precisely why, Rigter places the upper limit at 10,000.[159]

The suggestion of more recent commentators that the cases of euthanasia in the Netherlands may be significantly higher—on the order of from 18,000 to 20,000—met with sharp dissent from Rigter and his colleague at the Health Council Dr. Els Borst-Eilers: "Look carefully at who says these things and you will see only two groups: journalists who want to be alarming so that they can sell stories, or people who are so fanatic that they oppose euthanasia no matter what the patient wants."[160] The mention by me of Richard Fenigsen, who has suggested that the number of cases of euthanasia is perhaps double what has been suggested, drew a rebuke: "Foreigners always look first at these extreme claims, but there is no basis for such an estimate. The man has no data, and he could not produce such data, because [such numbers] do not exist. No one in the Netherlands believes Fenigsen, because such a thing [as he suggests] could not happen here."[161]

Fenigsen's sources, in addition to personal experiences (which he documents with names, places, and dates), are found in several places but do lean heavily on the writings of C. I. Dessaur and C. J. C. Rutenfrans, a criminologist and lawyer, respectively, at the University of Nijmegen.[162] These latter two authors do not present empirical studies to bolster their claims but cite estimates given to them "by supporters of euthanasia."[163] Dessaur and Rutenfrans give a range of from 6,000 to 12,000 cases of euthanasia per year, and others (most notably Fenigsen) claim that the number is even higher. In defense of the numbers he cites, Fenigsen submits the following observation:

> Getting a precise number is not so hard as the government would want outsiders to believe; they can do it, but it takes some effort. I think they do not want to [study] euthanasia so carefully, because of what they might be forced [to conclude]. Besides, these numbers are not *ours* [that is, from those opposed to euthanasia], but from people who believe the practice should be legitimate, and who are on the "inside" of things here. If my numbers are so wrong, then let them show how [they are wrong]. They certainly have the power and the money to do this.[164]

Fenigsen's protests and his other documentation of abuses of the practice notwithstanding, one would struggle, given current research into this problem, to justify the higher estimates of the practice. Even if one assumes that the Hague and Amsterdam surveys underestimated the practice (because they surveyed only general practitioners) and one adds Admiraal's estimate of another 1,000 cases, the total comes to approximately 6,000 cases per year—the lower end of the estimate by Dessaur and Rutenfrans.

Thus, the available information on the prevalence of this practice leaves one in an unsatisfying position. If it is true that the higher figures cited by Fenigsen and others opposed to euthanasia reflect their particular biases, it is equally true that others who find the practice permissible have an interest in demonstrating that euthanasia is practiced infrequently, that it is, in fact, a method of last recourse. I pointed out to Rigter, for example, that his statement that euthanasia accounts for "about 2% of deaths that occur in general practice in the Netherlands," which he and his colleagues published in the *British Medical Journal,* was misleading and that in private he suggests a higher and broader range of prevalence. He replied that in any case, all of these numbers were opinions and that one estimate was, technically, as valid as another.

Irrespective of how much credence one chooses to place in any of these estimates, it should be noted that many have made their way into popular and professional magazines and journals.[165] Moreover, when estimates are given, they rarely place the numbers in any context, which can be deceiving or misleading. The lowest estimate (from the Ministry of Justice) would suggest that euthanasia accounts for less than 0.2% of deaths in the Netherlands in any given year.[166] The highest estimate I have seen (published in a right-to-life organization newsletter, *Pro Vita*) suggests 20,000 cases, which would account for a staggering 16.5% of the mortality rate in the Netherlands.[167] The middle estimates—those suggested by Admiraal and Rigter—would suggest that euthanasia accounts for from 4% to 8% of deaths. Beyond these estimates, the prevalence of euthanasia in the Netherlands remains unknown. It goes without saying, moreover, that the epidemiologic data that would further characterize the patient population receiving euthanasia (age, gender, underlying pathology, and so on) are also unknown.

"What we have right now," to echo Mr. Sutorius's comment, is a practice that seems to have taken hold in the Netherlands but which no one can precisely describe. The evidence on the clinical aspect of this practice that has appeared in print has been almost exclusively of an anecdotal nature (selected clinical vignettes, for example) or has had limited generalizability.[168] Moreover, it is a practice on whose broad outlines there appears to be some consensus, but it is a peculiarly fragile consensus that seems to disintegrate when it comes to specifics. Formally forbidden, though tolerated in practice, it seems to have become part of the political and legal landscape in the Netherlands, although one would be at a loss to give precise details of how and how often euthanasia occurs.

I noted in the preface to this study that in following the arguments on both sides of this issue, I encountered no one who had yet described the practice of euthanasia with any precision. And so I asked the basic question, What does this practice of euthanasia look like? This simplistic-sounding question has no simple answer, for the practice, as I subsequently found, is as varied as the personalities and problems of the patients who ask for euthanasia. Still, the absence of verifiable data in the literature—and the contradictory conclusions drawn from the same evidence—led me to focus more narrowly on the actual practice of euthanasia. In the following section, I describe how I explored this problem and gathered data from the best of all sources—the people who practice euthanasia.

— 3 —

Describing the Practice of Euthanasia: Questions, Methods, and Case Studies

> In a decision to honor a request for euthanasia, the point of departure has always been that the doctor and the patient must stand with their backs to the wall, that is to say, that they no longer see any possibility of making the suffering of the patient bearable.[1]

EUTHANASIA IN ACTION: QUESTIONS AND METHODS

What does it mean to say that euthanasia in the Netherlands is permitted only when the patient and physician stand "with their backs to the wall?" What does it mean, in particular, in the fluid state of affairs that now exists in the Netherlands? That it is, ideally, to be a rare occurrence is clear. Prevalence is one matter, however, clinical practice another. Even if one could establish precisely how often euthanasia occurs in the Netherlands, it would still leave unanswered how the practice is realized and how well it conforms to the norms established by the courts and professional organizations in the Netherlands. A well-regulated and clearly defined practice of euthanasia (irrespective of how often it occurs) seems to be the concern of most defenders of the practice.[2] Alternatively, even a relatively few cases of *involuntary* euthanasia, for example, would be cause for alarm.[3]

What is lacking in the literature is precisely the details of the practice that would give substance to the generally vague guidelines. Apart from the handful of court cases published in the Netherlands between 1981 and the present, what generally finds its way into print are hypothetical cases or cases by individual practitioners or their associates.[4] Almost absent altogether are series of cases or a systematic evaluation of the details of the practice on a large scale.[5] Moreover, what has appeared in print leaves unanswered questions that I thought were important before undertaking this study (irrespective of whether or not one considers euthanasia permissible).

Specifically, it seemed important to understand how clinicians interpreted the guidelines for euthanasia in practice, whether the guidelines were consistently applied from case to case (for a particular physician), and whether there was disagreement between physicians and others involved in making these decisions on what was permissible euthanasia. Thus, I came to this portion of the study with the following questions:

1. How is the phrase "intolerable suffering" interpreted by clinicians and others responsible for agreeing to assist in suicide?
2. How is the request to die determined to be stable and enduring?
3. How do physicians present alternatives to the patient's request, so that the patient has a reasonable understanding of other solutions to his or her problem?
4. Are there consistent criteria for determining that the request is voluntary? Do clinicians consider a patient's cognitive and affective status a part of the voluntariness of the request? If so, are there standard ways of determining this?
5. How is the decision to honor a request for euthanasia made, who is consulted, and how is the decision-making process documented?
6. What is the actual clinical practice of euthanasia; that is, what protocols are followed, what drugs are given, and how do the clinicians themselves describe the event?
7. Who is present when the patient is euthanized?
8. How is the death certificate written up, and when, if ever, is the public prosecutor notified?
9. How do clinicians view this practice? For example, do they worry about its abuse? Do they worry for their own legal standing when they practice euthanasia?

The list of questions is long and involved, but it seemed to me that they were the sort of questions that could be answered, in part, by having clinicians describe, in detail, the case histories of patients whom they had euthanized. Some of the answers—the patient's request for euthanasia, for example, or the patient's cognitive status—would be a part of a thorough clinical history; other answers would evolve during the case presentation and with further probing. More importantly, these are the sorts of details that might illuminate the private side of this practice: how physicians and patients themselves interpret the limits of euthanasia. The best source for this information, obviously, is the participants in the practice. For obvious reasons, this data necessarily had to come from the physicians.

In January 1989, I arranged to spend a month in Amsterdam and stayed at the Free University of Amsterdam. I used the hospitality of this institution as a base from which to make contact with physicians, government officials, and others involved in the euthanasia debate. In the following section, I discuss the selection of physicians, the nature and structure of the interviews, and the collection of information. The data from this process—twenty-six case studies—appear immediately afterward. Finally, I conclude this chapter with a summary of the cases and a discussion of the limitations of this approach. The evaluation and analysis of the information gathered from the interviews follows in Chapter 4.

FINDING THE PHYSICIANS

In preparation for the study, I had written to two organizations in the Netherlands, the KNMG and the NVVE, requesting assistance with the project. I had reasoned (incorrectly, as it turned out) that the most likely sources of information on the actual practice of euthanasia might be found through the physicians' professional organization (the KNMG) and the organization most vocal in changing the laws prohibiting euthanasia (the NVVE). Additionally, I had written or telephoned a number other contacts—including physicians, lawyers, and health officials—with the same request. Specifically, I had asked for general information on their (or their organization's) position on euthanasia; further, I had asked if either they or someone in the organization would know how to contact physicians willing to speak on the practice of euthanasia.[6] The KNMG responded only with a copy of their official statement on euthanasia, which had already appeared in *Medisch Contact:* they made no mention of my other request. The NVVE was more forthcoming, providing not only information but also suggesting that they would be able to put me in contact with a number of physicians willing to speak on the subject. On my arrival in the Netherlands, however, the NVVE's offer became more tentative. They could, perhaps, give me the phone number of one physician they knew, but they would have to speak to him first. I had to understand, said one official (who requested anonymity), that they could not know if I was "friendly" or "unfriendly."[7] In either case, they did put me in touch with their foreign secretary, William Roose, who subsequently suggested some names whom I might want to call, he said, but who might not be willing to talk.

With my other contacts, I experienced the same initial guardedness but managed to collect in total a list of sixteen physicians. Of that number, seven declined outright to be interviewed.[8] Of the remaining nine, two called back after initially agreeing to be interviewed, and canceled. Five of the remaining seven were interviewed alone; one left the interview shortly after it began because of a hospital emergency and called in the nurse on the ward to complete the interview. The remaining physician was interviewed as part of the "terminal team" in the hospital that handled cases of euthanasia. In addition to these seven medical sources, I found two nonmedical sources of information that I decided to include for specific reasons. One, the relative of a man who had been euthanized, had helped care for the man during his last months and had very detailed information on his brother's clinical case. The second, an ethicist at a university hospital, was part of a consulting team on euthanasia and also had excellent notes on two cases of euthanasia.

In total, then, there were nine separate sources of clinical information on cases of euthanasia included in this study. They are listed in Table 3. For obvious reasons, neither the interviewees nor the locale are named. Each source is identified with a letter (from A to I, in the chronological order in which the sources were interviewed), which matches the clinical information gathered from that source (I destroyed the code sheet at the end of the study). Beyond this, the sources are identified only by their profession or their relationship to the person discussed in the cases, the number of cases they discussed, and the date and place (hospital or office) where the interview occurred. In subsequent discussions, the physicians will be further identified as either general practitioners or specialists. The terminal-care team (Source I) consisted of an attending physician, a general ward nurse, and one of the chaplains in the hospital.

TABLE 3 Sources of Information on Cases of Euthanasia

Code	Profession or Relationship	No. of Cases	Date and Place of Interview
A	Physician	5	1/17/89, hospital
B	Physician	3	1/20/89, office
C	Nurse	2	1/23/89, hospital
D	Physician	4	1/23/89, hospital
E	Relative of deceased	1	1/25/89, office
F	Physician	4	1/24/89, hospital
G	Bioethicist	2	1/25/89, hospital
H	Physician	2	1/26/89, hospital
I	Terminal-care team	3	1/26/89, hospital

THE STRUCTURE OF THE INTERVIEWS

When contacted for interviews, the respondents were assured of confidentiality. Neither the patients whom they described, nor they themselves, nor the institution or city in which they worked would be identified in the study. To further assure them of my intentions, and of the bounds of the study, I offered to give each a phone number (to the University of Chicago Department of General Medicine) that they could call at my expense to verify my credentials. None of the respondents did so.

To the first set of interviews (those conducted on January 17 and January 20, 1989) I brought a portable tape recorder and asked the interviewees if I could tape the interviews (with the assurance that the tapes would be used to verify my notes and that they would be erased immediately afterward). In both cases they declined. Their reasons for declining suggested to me that this information was even more sensitive than I had first believed and that the tape recorder was considered intrusive and potentially dangerous.[9] I did not bring the tape recorder to subsequent interviews.

Originally, I had intended to structure the interviews around two sets of questions. One set contained the guidelines on euthanasia set out by previous court opinions and by the KNMG. Because the guidelines are found in so many different places and in such varying language, I modified one recent version of the guidelines found in English. The version of the guidelines used appears in Table 4. Because of the uncertainty that still exists about the specifics of the guidelines, I further tested the applicability of my version with knowledgeable people in three fields: a health official, a bioethicist, and a physician.[10] Each was asked to read the version to see if it faithfully reflected the consensus on permissible euthanasia. With little dissent, they agreed that the version I presented to them was representative of the established consensus.[11]

A second set of questions, which would have more formally structured the interviews, was discarded for several reasons. The instrument was long and was written with the assumption that the interviews would be taped (so that asides, elaborations, and other

TABLE 4 Guidelines for Euthanasia Used in Interviews[13]

1. There must be psychological or physical suffering that is said to be intolerable by the supplicant himself/herself.

2. The experience of suffering and the desire to die must be durable and persistent.

3. The decision to die must be established to be completely voluntary on the part of the patient/supplicant.

4. The supplicant must have a reasonable understanding of his or her situation and of the possible alternatives; he or she must be in such a state as to weigh the options and alternatives and must have completed this process upon requesting to die.

5. There is no other reasonable solution apparent to improve the situation for the supplicant.

6. There must be consultation with at least one other physician on the permissibility of a particular case of euthanasia.

7. Euthanasia must be administered by a physician, and the task may not be delegated to a nonphysician.

8. There must be no unnecessary suffering brought upon others involved.

9. With the decision to assist to die, as well as with the performance of the act itself, the greatest possible care must be involved.

10. Note of the fact that euthanasia occurred should be documented either in the death certificate or with the public prosecutor's office.

subtleties of the interview could be captured by other means while I attended to filling in the questionnaire). When it became obvious that the interviewees would resist being tape recorded (or decline to be interviewed altogether), the structured format became cumbersome and intrusive.[12] Moreover, it became readily apparent that on a topic as sensitive as this, I would be able to gather more and fuller information by giving the interviewees more latitude to tell their stories. What might have been gained in terms of consistent instrumentation across all cases (by using a tightly structured format) would have been more than offset, I decided, by the loss of cooperation on the part of some or by guarded responses on the part of others. Moreover, given the formal illegality of what was being described to me, and the difficulty I encountered in finding reliable sources willing to share information, it seemed prudent to adapt my original strategy to avoid obstacles I had not anticipated.[14]

Thus, the format I did follow in the interviews was a good deal more flexible.[15] I asked the interviewees to describe, if possible, three cases of euthanasia in which they had been personally involved during the previous five years. I told them to present the case as they would if giving a clinical case history and asked them to include as many details as they felt were pertinent. Two physicians (Sources A and D) initially objected to this format, because, as one said, "these are not typical case histories; one is not doing what is normally done." Nevertheless I persisted, and asked them to structure the cases as much as possible along clinical lines, assuring them that they were free to add any other details they felt were necessary to describe the case adequately. For Sources E and G (the relative of a patient who was euthanized and a bioethicist), I asked each to relate the cases with as much detail as possible.

I let each interviewee speak, uninterrupted, while presenting each case, and I took notes while they spoke. When they finished describing the case, I read back to them what I had noted, asking each time if I had accurately recorded what they had said. I made changes in the case notes where people pointed out errors or ambiguities, or where they felt that their original story needed further elaboration.

After each case presentation had been noted, reread, and amended as indicated, I then asked for clarification on points about which I was still unsure or which had been left out of the narrative altogether. Some questions were simply an attempt to elicit elaborations on particular details of the case.[16] Others were an attempt to reconcile what I perceived as inconsistencies in the narrative.[17] Finally, the follow-up on the case histories invariably ended with a series of questions on the guidelines for euthanasia. In some instances, many of the points of the guidelines had already been addressed in the case histories. For example, one set of interviews (Source I, the terminal-care team), seemed to have collectively memorized the guidelines and made specific note of particular requirements while narrating the cases. In other instances, however, I would press more vigorously for explanation when I felt a guideline had been ignored or misinterpreted. Thus, for example, when it seemed from the case narratives that a patient was depressed, I called into question whether the requirement of "voluntariness" stipulated by the protocol had been followed. In some cases, the respondents would add details that they had left out of the earlier narrative. In others, the respondents would say that they did not remember. In still others, it became obvious that particular points had been either overlooked or not sufficiently considered.

I should mention here that these last portions of the interviews, where I probed into matters of judgment and professional care, became in some instances tense, and in two sets of interviews, they were characterized by outright hostility (Sources B and G). In fact, the relative brevity of the information gathered from these two sources is due, in part, to what were perceived as hostile questions.[18] Whether it was the nature of the subject or persistent or tactless queries on my part is unclear. Others who were as extensively questioned seemed relatively composed by comparison.

At the end of each interview, the cases were summarized and put into a standard format. The twenty-six cases, which are collected in the next section of this chapter, are ordered in sequence, as the interviews occurred. In each case, the patient summary is identified simply by a numeral (1 through 26) and the code letter for the source (A through I).

CASE STUDY SUMMARIES

Case 1 (Source A)

The patient was a 67-year-old man with a long history of alcoholism. He had worked as a laborer in the dockyards near Rotterdam until approximately six years ago, when increasingly poor health and his erratic behavior forced his retirement. The patient was divorced and had no children. He had received medical care from the local general practitioner for the previous eleven years for his recurring bouts of pneumonia, which became increasingly complicated by the patient's heavy drinking. The GP [general practitioner] had referred the patient to a specialist at this hospital twice for ascites, once for pneumonia.

Final admission to the hospital came when the GP noticed the patient's jaundiced complexion, coupled with the patient's complaints of increasing fatigue, weight loss, and cramping pain in the stomach. Examination and diagnostic tests at the hospital were suggestive of malignancy. Subsequent surgery revealed metastatic hepatocellular cancer; part of the tumor obstructing the bile duct was removed, but the rest of the tumor was deemed inoperable.

The patient was tried on one round of chemotherapy; there was some temporary relief of symptoms. The patient refused a second round ("said he had too much nausea, fatigue"). Pain was controlled "fairly well—when he complained of pain, we increased the dosage [of morphine]."

Following the initial chemotherapy treatment, the patient's condition deteriorated rapidly. The medical team suggested placement in a nursing home (for palliative, hospice care). The patient refused ("he said he did not want to go someplace new"). The patient asked for the GP in order to discuss his case; after consultation, the patient requested euthanasia.

The case was referred to a "terminal care" team. A psychiatrist was sent to talk with the patient; the psychiatrist said the patient was noncooperative and that he denied depression. The patient repeated the request for euthanasia "almost every day." The medical team suggested "several alternatives—we could, for instance, continue increasing the narcotics slowly; we also tried to see if he would try another [chemotherapy] protocol." Patient refused alternatives. After the final set of refusals, the team decided to wait another week "to be sure."

At the end of the waiting period, the request was granted (the patient again refused psychiatric evaluation).

A date was set for euthanasia (the day after the waiting period imposed by the team, and "before breakfast"). The patient was offered an oral "euthanatic" but preferred to have the agent administered to him. He did not request pastoral care or counseling. Early on the morning, the physician from the team and the head nurse entered. An IV [intravenous line] containing 1 gram of pentobarbital in a 500-milliliter solution was begun. The patient became drowsy, "seemed to sleep." At the end of the IV ("about one hour") a second IV with 2 grams in a 500-milliliter solution was begun. The patient stopped breathing approximately twenty minutes after administration of the second IV. The physician pronounced death. The death certificate entered "heart failure" as the cause of death. The same diagnosis was entered in the chart. The prosecutor was not notified.

Case 2 (Source A)

A 35-year-old woman was admitted for the fourth time to this hospital to be treated for complications arising from amyotrophic lateral sclerosis (ALS). She was single, and until four years before, had been working as a music teacher at a local school.

After being diagnosed with the disease, she worked part-time at the school and "tried some exercises and therapy." She also moved back in with her parents. The disease seemed to progress slowly for the first two years, then her condition deteriorated rapidly. She continued to live with her family, even after she became incapable of bathing, dressing, or performing other routine activities.

The possibility of euthanasia arose during her first admission (for pneumonia). During the initial interview, the patient expressed her desire not to live "on a machine" and "asked not to suffer." The parents later repeated their daughter's request to the physician and staff. The staff followed up on the discussion by asking the patient to be more specific, and she said that she preferred euthanasia to life on a respirator. At each subsequent hospitalization, she reaffirmed this request. "Her big fear was no air . . . not having enough air and a machine to breathe for her. . . . I said I understand . . . and she had nothing to fear."

Rapidly deteriorating pulmonary function precipitated her final admission. The patient was placed on oxygen and given morphine. The physician told her that she would probably need to be placed on a respirator this time: "the oxygen was already very high, and she hardly got enough. . . . I asked again about euthanasia." The patient assented, then assented again when her family was present. The case was taken to the terminal-care committee, and the request was approved ("No one wanted to wait . . . we knew the patient.") No psychiatric evaluation was ordered. The physician informed the patient of the decision; the patient and her family asked for a couple of days "to get things together. . . . I think to get used to the idea." The hospital chaplain came in frequently to be with her and the family.

The day before the euthanasia was to take place, the patient's pulmonary function deteriorated even further. The patient and family decided that waiting the additional day was unbearable. That evening, the family (both parents and one brother and his wife), the physician, the nurse, and the chaplain gathered around the patient's bed. The family said their good-byes, "made a prayer with the pastor," and left to wait outside. The physician began an IV drip of 1 gram pentobarbital in a 500-milliliter solution; as soon as the patient was unconscious, he administered 4 milligrams intravenously of a curare derivative (metocurine iodide?). Respiration ceased "within a few seconds." Approximately five minutes later, the physician pronounced the patient dead. The cause of death was listed as "sudden respiratory arrest," and the public prosecutor was not notified. Orderlies were called in to clean and arrange the body, and then the family was brought back into the room.

Case 3 (Source A)

An 86-year-old woman had been residing in a nursing home for the past six years. She had been widowed for nine years and had continued to live at home until a broken hip necessitated nursing care. She had three children, two of whom lived near the nursing home and with whom she was close.

The patient had only "partially recovered" from the hip fracture. "Sometimes she used the cane, but mostly she used a wheelchair." The physician had known her as an inpatient "maybe three times" for treatment of recurring pneumonia. (The patient had a fifty-year history of regular cigarette smoking, and was also suffering from emphysema.)

Her previous admission to the hospital "was bad . . . she had deteriorated. . . . I think she was tired." The subject of euthanasia arose on this previous admission. "She said no more, and this was after she was cured. I had explained to her that each new bout was going to be worse." The patient then told the doctor that the next time she had to be brought in she wanted euthanasia.

Her final admission was also precipitated by pneumonia. "I wanted to do it in the nursing home, but they wouldn't let me do it there. She was very bad off, and they wanted her 'stabilized' first. . . . Silly, but I had no choice."

The family had been informed by both the patient and the doctor of the patient's request, and they concurred with the decision. At the onset of the final illness, the patient was brought in unresponsive.

"The doctor at the nursing home had already started therapy, but so what." The family was notified by the nursing home that the patient had been transferred.

The patient's daughter spoke with the physician, reminding him of her mother's request (which had been noted in her chart during the previous hospitalization.) "The decision had really already been made . . . the last time she came in, I talked with the terminal-care committee, because I didn't think she was going to recover. When she came in again, they already knew the case well." The following day, the patient was a bit more responsive, "she opened her eyes, talked to her daughter a little bit, took some food."

The physician does not remember the vital signs or symptoms in this final admission. "I already knew what we were going to do . . . psychiatric evaluation was pointless here, and we had already talked with her." After speaking with the daughter, the physician obtained permission to perform euthanasia the following day.

The physician and nurse were present (the daughter and son had asked only to be notified of the time, so that they could be at the hospital). The physician administered 1 gram of pentobarbital in a 500-milliliter infusion; a second infusion of 2 grams was administered ninety minutes later. Approximately thirty minutes after the final infusion, the patient ceased breathing. The physician pronounced death and entered "respiratory arrest" as the cause of death. The family was notified, and they arrived at the hospital within the hour.

Case 4 (Source A)

The patient was a 72-year-old woman with a long history of cigarette smoking. She was widowed (six years), and lived alone in a rented apartment. She had three children, all of whom lived near her and with whom she enjoyed a good relationship. With the exception of arthritis and infrequent bouts of bronchitis, she had been in relatively good health until two years previous, when she developed a persistent cough that lasted several weeks. Her family physician treated her, as before, with a cough suppressant. The patient complained of fatigue, and as the cough worsened, he referred her to this hospital for evaluation.

A chest X-ray disclosed a large density over the left lower lobe of a lung. She was kept in the hospital for further tests, including sputum cytology, which revealed the presence of malignant squamous cells. Histopathology revealed malignancy in the left lung (which was resected), as well as hilar node involvement. The patient was started on a regimen of chemotherapy and was discharged from the hospital approximately three weeks later.

The patient remained fairly stable for approximately seven months, then began to deteriorate. Her physicians at the hospital told her that the malignancy was widely disseminated, and they recommended a new protocol (chemotherapy and radiation). The regimen brought only minor relief, and after a few weeks, the patient complained of the side effects of the therapy, including fatigue, nausea, and the loss of almost all of her hair. The patient continued with the regimen a few more months, then asked that it be discontinued ("she said she wasn't going to get better, and this was worse").

After discontinuing the protocol, she returned to the care of her GP, who helped manage the pain medication at home. A daughter stayed with her during the day, and the other two children took turns staying the day. At some point during this phase in her illness, the subject of euthanasia was discussed (the family doctor made note of the conversation and related to the narrating physician that the three children were present). The patient said that there was going to come a time when it "should end," and she wanted it to be quickly. The family doctor said that he was uncomfortable doing euthanasia himself (he said he had no experience) but that he would help her when the time came.

Approximately a month later, the family physician contacted the hospital, requesting admission for the patient, who was developing severe dyspnea and whose pain he was having difficulty controlling. The patient was admitted to the oncology ward of the hospital and was placed on higher dosages of morphine and analgesics; she was also given phenothiazines to control the nausea and vomiting that had developed.

Shortly after the patient was admitted, the family physician requested a consult with the hospital attending physician, at which time the GP related the patient's conversations about euthanasia. The attending physician then spoke with the patient, who reaffirmed the request. The doctor asked for permission to speak with other members of the family; all three children asserted that their mother wanted euthanasia, and they were in full agreement with her wishes. The terminal-care team was contacted for an evaluation. A psychiatrist was sent, who suggested after evaluating the patient that she be placed on tricyclic antidepressants ("he said that she had been in pain for some time, and that we should try this course first"). The patient was placed on an antidepressant, and her pain regimen was modified. During this time, she continued to reiterate her request to the nurses, one of whom brought up the matter again with the terminal-care committee. The committee suggested waiting ("they wanted to see if the psychiatric drugs would work"). Approximately three weeks after starting the regimen, the patient's case came up again. The psychiatrist testified that the patient was still probably depressed; not being able to say whether the medication would alleviate her symptoms, the psychiatrist suggested waiting. One of the nurses said that the patient was fully in control of her senses and that waiting would do no good. The committee decided to wait another week.

At the end of the week, the patient—who continued to press her request—said that the pain was better controlled but that she was "tired of all of this." Her case came up again in the committee, which agreed to her request. After being notified of approval, the patient asked her family to come to discuss the decision. The family was in full agreement and made it a point to speak with the staff afterward to confirm their mother's choice.

The following day, the attending physician and the patient agreed to euthanasia that evening. The family was called to the hospital that afternoon. The hospital chaplain (who had been seeing the patient, and who spoke on her behalf at the terminal-care conference) said a brief liturgy, then left with the family to wait outside.

The attending physician then began an infusion of 1 gram of pentobarbital in a 500-milliliter solution. A second infusion (2 grams in 500-milliliters) was started within the hour. The patient had fallen unconscious, and her respirations became shallow and slowed. The physician then injected 4 milligrams of a curare derivative. Within a minute, the patient's breathing ceased. The physician waited a few more minutes, then declared death. "Respiratory arrest" was entered as the cause of death; the prosecutor was not notified. After the patient was cleaned and arranged, the family was brought in with the hospital chaplain.

Case 5 (Source A)

The patient was an 88-year-old widow ("for more than twenty years") who had been residing in a nursing home for the past nine years. For the previous five years or so, the staff at the nursing home had heard the patient say that she wanted to die, "that she didn't want to live like this anymore." She had suffered a stroke just prior to entering the nursing home, from which she was only partially recovered: she suffered total left hemiparesis, was wheelchair-bound, and still slurred her speech to a significant degree. She had had one child, who had died the previous year. Following the death of this child, the nursing home staff noted that the patient became even more withdrawn and antisocial. She quit performing most grooming activities (when placed in a tub, for example, she would bathe herself with minimal help, but now refused to bathe at all or to brush her hair) and would periodically refuse to eat. The medical director of the nursing home called this physician at the local hospital, with a request that she be transferred "for observation" ("really, he wanted to know if the patient was a candidate for euthanasia").

The patient's repeated requests for euthanasia brought her to the attention of the physician relating the case. He reviewed the patient's chart and called the nursing home director to verify the facts. He then presented the patient's case to the terminal-care committee. The committee agreed that there had been a long-standing request for euthanasia but waited for further psychological evaluation.

What further evaluation took place at this point is unclear, but after approximately one month in the hospital, the patient was euthanized. As with previous patients under this physician's care, he used 1 gram of pentobarbital, followed by 4 milligrams of tubocurarine (she did not need a second infusion of pentobarbital to render her unconscious). "Respiratory arrest" was entered on the death certificate; the public prosecutor was not notified.

Case 6 (Source B)

The patient, a 78-year-old man, had been in the care of his family doctor for more than four years when he was diagnosed with colon cancer ("he had been having pain, passing bloody stools"). By the time the cancer was diagnosed, the cancer was widely metastasized to other organs in his abdomen, including his liver. Several rounds of chemotherapy failed to cure him or to palliate his symptoms to a significant degree. Approximately one year after starting the chemotherapy, the patient brought up the subject of euthanasia with the physician. The patient had already been told that his disease was fatal, and he had become fatigued from the chemotherapy (which he did not tolerate well).

The family doctor suggested discontinuation of therapy at the hospital and started giving the patient "large amounts of pain medication." The patient seemed happier with this alternative regimen, but after approximately one month, he brought up the question of euthanasia again. The family doctor spoke with both the patient and his wife, and both were agreed that if the patient's end was to be as slow and painful as the previous year, they both preferred euthanasia. The parent's contacted their two children, each of whom in turn spoke with the doctor. After hearing the doctor's prognosis, both children agreed with their father's decision.

Approximately "six or seven" weeks after this final request ("the patient needed some time to arrange matters"), the doctor performed euthanasia at the patient's home. The wife and two children were in attendance and had already said their farewells. The doctor asked the patient once more if this was what he wanted, and the patient said yes. The doctor gave the patient a mixed solution of orphenadrine (Norflex) and a phenobarbital (the doctor did not give the dosages of each). The patient lost consciousness within a few minutes; after twenty minutes, his breathing became labored; after forty minutes, the physician pronounced him dead.

The physician then stayed with the family to provide support and to await the arrival of the ambulance. The public prosecutor was not notified. "Cardiac arrest" was entered on the death certificate as the proximate cause of death.

Case 7 (Source B)

The patient was an 89-year-old widow, who lived by herself. She had suffered a stroke six years previously, from which she had partially recuperated. She came in to this doctor's care shortly after her return from the hospital when she moved to a smaller house in another neighborhood. She had, since her return, become increasingly unable to care for herself. For "about three years," she had asked the doctor about euthanasia and once had threatened to kill herself if the doctor did not accede to her request. The doctor had suggested psychotherapy, which she declined, and at one point the doctor tried her on anti-depressant medication ("which I am never sure she would take"). The family doctor had contacted the visiting nurse in the area asking her to visit this patient on a regular basis. The GP had also arranged for the local welfare department to send a part-time aide to help the patient with cooking and heavier tasks. The patient's mood would lift periodically, but she mentioned euthanasia "almost every time she would visit me."

The woman's requests became so persistent that the doctor agreed to accede if she told a son (who lived a good distance away). The woman refused and said her son had nothing to do with this matter. The patient then called a neighbor, who came with the patient to visit the physician. The neighbor helped the woman plead her case and suggested that if this doctor would not perform euthanasia, the neighbor would help the patient find another doctor who would. The doctor finally agreed and, a week later, euthanized the patient in her home (no one else was present) by giving her a solution of orphenadrine and pentobarbital to drink. She died within the half hour after drinking the solution. The doctor then notified the son that evening that his mother had passed away suddenly but did not tell him of the circumstances. The cause of death was listed as "cardiac arrest"; the public prosecutor was not notified.

Case 8 (Source B)

The patient, who was 86 years old, had told his physician repeatedly that if he became demented, he wanted euthanasia. He had seen too many of his friends lose their minds, he said, and did not want to live out his existence in a nursing home or become a burden to his wife. The doctor had taken note of this request in the patient's chart and had discussed the matter with the patient's wife. During the year prior to his demise, the patient became increasingly concerned about bouts of forgetfulness and asked the doctor if he had "Alzheimer or am I losing my mind." The doctor told him that such changes were to be expected with age.

Three months prior to his death, the patient contracted pneumonia, which required hospitalization. After the patient's discharge, the doctor said that the patient complained increasingly about the state of his health. A few weeks before the patient's death, one of the patient's sons came to the doctor and said that his father had been talking increasingly about euthanasia; he asked if this was "really a possibility." The doctor arranged a meeting with the family to discuss the issue. At the meeting, the patient reiterated that, rather than becoming demented (which he felt was slowly happening to him), he wanted euthanasia. He also made it clear that he did not want further hospitalization. The physician "listened a lot, but I made no recommendations."

Approximately one week before the patient's death, he came down again with pneumonia and refused hospitalization. The doctor suggested a course of antibiotics, which the patient also refused. A few days later, the patient's wife called back and said that her husband was "in a bad way." When the doctor arrived at the patient's home, he found the patient "awake, but very angry; he said he was tired of this and wanted it over." Given the patient's previous requests, the doctor asked the wife what should be done; the wife was unable to give a consistent answer. The son was called, and after talking to his father, told the physician that "this is truly what he wants." The physician suggested waiting one more day, but the patient refused. The wife finally agreed that her husband's wishes should be met. The doctor left to finish some office calls.

Later that night, the doctor returned and again asked the patient if he wanted euthanasia. The patient said yes and said that "even now my wife agrees." The son, also present, agreed with the father's request. The doctor then prepared the euthanatic. With son and wife in attendance, the patient drank a solution of orphenadrine and pentobarbital. He expired within forty-five minutes. The doctor called an ambulance and told the attendants that the patient had died of cardiac arrest. The public prosecutor was not notified.

Case 9 (Source C)

(NOTE: The physician in charge of this case, who started to narrate the history, was interrupted. A nurse who was present on this case and on Case 10 completed the narratives.) The patient was a 62-year-old man with widely metastasized lung cancer. He had tried both a partial lung resection and radiation therapy. After his previous hospitalization, he had been discharged home to the care of his family doctor, with a regimen to help control pain.

During his previous hospitalization, the patient's case had been discussed by the terminal-care team because the subject of euthanasia had been brought up by the patient's family (that it was the family that brought up the subject was reiterated twice by the narrator). One representative of the team had spoken with the patient, who said that unless the pain could be better controlled, he did not want to undergo any more therapy. The representative acknowledged having understood, and wanted to know if the patient had actually requested euthanasia (again, the narrator emphasized that the terminal-care team was concerned that the request come from the patient). The patient had "told me (the nurse) that if that was the only solution, that is what he wanted." He said the same thing to the terminal-care team.

After "maybe a few weeks," the patient was readmitted to the hospital for pain control. "He was very uncomfortable and said that this should not go on any further." The physician switched regimens, but the patient wanted some assurance from the nurse that his pain would disappear: "But no one can give such a promise; I told him we would do everything possible."

Shortly after the regimen was switched, the patient made another request for euthanasia. "This was a case of extreme emergency; he really was in great pain." Given that the patient's request had been previously documented, the terminal-care team approved the request. While the patient's family waited outside ("I do not remember how many were there, but I do know it was quite a few people"), an IV drip of pentobarbital was started; when the patient became unconscious, another drip was begun. In the middle of the second drip, an injection of potassium chloride was administered into the IV line. [When pressed about this latter detail, the nurse looked startled and read from the case notes again; it said potassium chloride, but the nurse did not remember precisely what drug was given.] The patient suffered a cardiac arrest "very quickly." The nurse arranged the body, then called in the family. She does not know how the death certificate was filled out, but is "very sure" that the prosecutor for the district was not notified.

Case 10 (Source C)

(NOTE: As in Case 9, this case was narrated by the nurse on the case.) The patient was a 79-year-old woman with multiple pathologies who had been in and out of this hospital for the past three years. Prior to her most recent admission, she had suffered a myocardial infarction. During her convalescence, she had told the cardiologist on the case that she did not want to be resuscitated if she had a cardiac arrest. A former nurse herself, the patient said that she "had been through too much already and knew what the future of such cases was." Her case was referred to the terminal-care team, who documented the request. During this consultation, however, the patient told one of the members that if she became comatose, she also wanted euthanasia. The case caused "great concern" because this formerly vigorous woman had withstood all the therapies to date quite stoically. Her attending physician spoke with her again and suggested that she talk with a psychiatrist. The psychiatrist's report suggested no sign of depression or other affective illness. The physician on the case made note of her request prior to discharging the patient to her daughter's home.

"A few months later," the patient was readmitted because of complaints of "difficulty breathing and much coughing." A diagnosis of congestive heart failure was established. After treatment was started and the patient's condition stabilized, she again brought up the subject of euthanasia to the nurse and said "that the time had come." The physician on the case verified the request and asked to contact the daughter. The daughter reaffirmed that this was what her mother wanted, and concurred in the decision. The physician requested another psychiatric consult. The psychiatrist this time reiterated that there were no overt signs of depression or loss of cognitive function but suggested waiting "about a week." At the end of the period, the patient, who had persisted in her request, asked that a decision be made, because if the hospital would not accede to the request, "she certainly knew doctors who would." Her case was brought up again before the terminal-care team, and the request was approved.

With the daughter present "and holding the hand of her mother," the physician began an infusion of pentobarbital; the patient lost consciousness quickly. The physician waited for the first IV to end, started another one, then shortly after, injected the patient with tubocurarine ("I do not know the doses here, but very little curare will do.") Five minutes or so afterward, the physician pronounced the patient dead. The nurse does not know how the death certificate was filled out but does know that the district prosecutor was not notified.

Case 11 (Source D)

An 82-year-old man was admitted to the hospital after a "very huge stroke." The patient's recovery was slow and "very unhappy, he was almost completely paralyzed on one side." A former lawyer, the patient had told his own family physician many times that he preferred death to the "slow death" he had seen his friends go through, and he had made the doctor promise to euthanize him should the time come: "I talked to this family doctor many times about this case; I talked to the man's wife and his children; everyone agreed that this is what he had wanted."

When the man regained his ability to communicate, the attending physician brought up his previous request (on this point, the doctor is quite clear): "The family during this time kept telling me that their father did not want such an existence, that he had talked many times about this; I had to ask the patient." The patient said that he wanted euthanasia, "that this was no way for a man to live." The attending physician again spoke with the family doctor, who reiterated the patient's previous request.

The attending physician then called the family to the hospital and, with the family in attendance, asked the patient when he wanted to be euthanized; the patient replied immediately. "I said yes, but asked for them to wait at least a day; sometimes when [the reality] of the event is on people, they change their minds." The following evening, with the wife and two children in attendance, the physician euthanized the patient using pentobarbital in an IV drip, followed by curare. "He died very quickly; he might well have died without the curare." The physician entered "cardiac arrest" on the death certificate but did notify the prosecutor.

The prosecutor waited until the following morning, then interviewed the physician and asked to see his notes. "There was no problem here; it was all documented, and he could also talk to the other doctor and the family." The district attorney did not prosecute.

Case 12 (Source D)

A 32-year-old man with AIDS had been admitted twice previously to this hospital: once for a persistent cough (during which time the diagnosis of AIDS was established), the second time for a bout of *pneumocystis carinii* pneumonia (from which he had recovered temporarily).

"This case I remember well because from the beginning the man said 'I want to die.' Right away, before we had started anything." The patient, who was estranged from his family, was accompanied to his hospital visits by his lover, and the hospital had accommodated their needs by giving them a private room: "In cases like this, we always try to make a difficult situation much easier; we always let the boyfriend stay in the hospital; it makes the patient better, less lonely."

During his previous admission (for pneumonia), the patient had requested euthanasia over the protests of his lover. The attending physician suggested a psychiatric consultation and at least a trial period of therapy. The psychiatrist concurred: "He said it was much too soon; maybe the desire to die came from the shock of this scary disease." The patient responded reasonably well to the treatment, but prior to discharge, he asked to speak alone to the doctor: "He said to me: 'This time, I am saved, but next time, no. I have seen this disease and prefer death.' What do you say to such a thing? Was he angry at me for saving his life?" The physician, as a precautionary measure, asked the psychiatrist and a member of the terminal-care team to speak to the patient before he was discharged: "These patients do not get better, only worse; he would be back, and then, it was necessary for someone else to know the problem here."

In fact, the patient returned "very soon, he was very ill and was brought by the boyfriend." Again, the patient brought up the desire to die and was emphatic about not starting treatment: "He said only drugs to make me feel better, not to cure." The physician contacted the terminal-care team, which sent a representative: "Not a doctor, but someone to put the request on paper." Shortly afterward ("the next morning") the request was approved: "But the problem was the boyfriend, who really needed some help too. Finally I said, 'If your friend wants this, if he is so sick, why do you act this way and make him suffer more?"

Over the lover's protests, the patient was euthanized that day by giving an oral euthanatic: "It is like an ice-cream mixture [milkshake]. I put in Norflex [orphenadrine] and pentobarbital, and then he drank it. Within the hour he was dead."

The prosecutor was notified "and took so much time with this case. I don't know if the boyfriend made accusations, but for several days, the prosecutor [kept] coming back. He asked if there was another doctor involved, and I said 'The whole hospital is involved,' but he wanted a name, so I said 'Talk to the hospital administrator, he can give the names of all the doctors here, just pick one.' " After a few weeks of deliberation, the prosecutor dropped the case.

Case 13 (Source D)

The patient, a 75-year-old woman, had been diagnosed with an inoperable brain tumor. Several rounds of radiation therapy had left her weakened. "She did not want anything else, and the doctor she had seen here had made a promise that if the radiotherapy did not work, she could have euthanasia." This promise took the form of an interview with the terminal-care team: "Before therapy, she wanted to be sure nothing would go too far; she already had lost her husband with cancer, and I think she was very afraid of what she had seen with his disease."

On the advice of her doctor, the terminal-care team agreed to the contract: "This is a case I do not understand very well; she was not my patient at the beginning, but only at the end. When I saw her, she was already very weak, and she asked, 'Are you the doctor that is going to end this?' " The physician consulted several times with the original doctor on the case and he also spoke with the terminal-care team. Before proceeding with the patient's request, the physician suggested that she speak with a psychiatrist; the patient declined. The physician then suggested that the family be called in, "but she said her family had died when her husband had died; the rest did not matter." The physician looked at the records of the terminal-care team, "and there were many written requests for euthanasia, and everyone on the committee said it was appropriate."

The patient was given an oral euthanatic (as in Case 12), and expired. The prosecutor who was called to the case did not even speak with the physician who performed the euthanasia but with the hospital administrator: "I was only asked by the administrator to sign some papers; this was very strange, but I believe now that the hospital has some agreement with the prosecutor."

Case 14 (Source D)

The patient was a 28-year-old woman with leukemia (the physician did not remember the specific type). She had been in remission for approximately one year, when she suffered a "cell explosion [blast crisis?]" and was brought to the hospital by her husband and her parents. During her remission, while she was at home, she and her husband had spoken with the family doctor "many times about euthanasia; this I am sure of . . . because I saw the doctor's records myself." The patient had indicated that if the remission failed, she did not want to undergo induction again (this is what I gather from the doctor's phrase "more cell replacement therapy") and did not want to linger in a hospital bed while she died.

Upon admission, she again declined therapy, and asked that her request be honored: "Why did not the family doctor do this? You see sometimes people who leave this responsibility to others; there is always the problem too of families who see death as something in a hospital, not the house." The terminal-care team interviewed the family doctor and the family and quickly approved the request. The patient's husband, parents, and family pastor were in the room when the physician first proffered an oral euthanatic: "This was a serious mistake on my behalf; she was really even too weak to keep the liquid in her mouth; it was an ugly event." The physician then started an IV drip of pentobarbital, and when the patient fell unconscious, the parents and pastor left the room, and the husband came to sit near her: "This case, with one who is so young, you remember very well; I went slowly, then after the rest had left, I told the husband, 'Now it is time,' and he kissed the hand of his wife and went outside." The physician then administered curare, and the patient died.

The prosecutor who investigated this case interviewed the physician and the family, "which was ridiculous, every time there are different rules," but subsequently the prosecutor dismissed the case.

Case 15 (Source E)

The case was narrated by a relative of a 59-year-old man who had an inoperable brain tumor. The patient's and narrator's families were very close, and the diagnosis of cancer in the patient was "like giving everybody in the family a disease of depression." The patient, an engineer by training, was the father of four children, the youngest of whom was just beginning to study at the university. "For more than a year, everybody's life became stopped; we would go to the hospital or go to his house, to help out, to see what was happening. The youngest child left school to come home; another child left a job to move back."

Somewhere in the "middle of this process," the patient began to discuss euthanasia. "It was a hopeless condition; he was dying, and the family was dying too." The rest of the family initially resisted the idea, but the patient persisted. "What changed the minds [of the other family members] was when we began to talk to his doctor: 'Is this hopeless? Will he suffer much? Do we need more medicine?' But the doctor was sure that nothing else would help." Another event that changed opinions was a visit to the hospital shortly before the patient died. "Such a terrible scene, with machines and tubes, his face was white, with no hair." The patient was discharged home: "The [family doctor] helped get him out."

Shortly after the patient returned home, the doctor brought up the issue of euthanasia: "It may seem a cruel thing, but it was the correct thing to do. [He] had asked many times for this, and now, all he could do was to wait in pain." The family, after this last traumatic visit to the hospital, agreed.

"It was very quick, very simple. We had gone to [his] room to be with him a few moments, then left [the wife] with [him] and the doctor. The rest of us waited outside, and then, maybe thirty minutes, they both came out. No noises, no screams. It was done with much dignity." Under the circumstances, the doctor did not call the prosecutor: "Really, this was a favor to us, but he asked that we also tell friends and the neighbors that he [the patient] had died in his sleep—so there would be no scandal—which was very easy, because everyone thought the end was soon to come."

Case 16 (Source F)

The case, "the worst one I had," according to the physician narrating the history, involved a 78-year-old woman in a nearby nursing home. The physician had been called by the nursing home director because the patient had gone into congestive heart failure (according to the medical director of the home). "I said to them, 'Bring her to the hospital.' But what they wanted was euthanasia." The physician went to examine the woman, who was indeed in heart failure and who told the physician she wanted to die. The physician examined her records, and there had been documentation over the past year of a request to die. "She said nothing was left for her: no husband, children who did not visit, a wheelchair. All she wanted was death." The physician suggested that the patient be moved to the hospital for observation and treatment, but the patient declined: " 'No more hospitals,' she said, all she wanted was to die." The physician then said that this was a matter for the nursing home to handle, but the home's director persisted: "They did not perform euthanasia [the director said], and the patient did not want to move. So, I said, it is allowed for me to kill her here, but not for you? Such hypocrisy."

The matter went to the administrator of the physician's hospital. [I note here that patients were often transferred back and forth between the two institutions; some patients who needed terminal, palliative care, for example, were moved to the nursing home to die.] "As a favor, he asked me, can you do this in the nursing home? It had become a great problem for the nursing home."

The physician acceded on the condition that the prosecutor be notified *in advance* of the procedure, something that the physician never did: "This is a place where euthanasia is not allowed, and here I was to do the euthanasia? What a problem if someone decided to call the police." As it was, the prosecutor—after speaking with the patient, the doctor, and the nursing home director—agreed that there were grounds for euthanasia and that he would not prosecute.

"Then, I go to do this as a favor, but I say, 'This is a suicide,' so that I can give oral drugs." The nursing home director, however, was afraid that an oral euthanatic would not accomplish the job: "[The director] says, 'Give her an injection,' because [the director] is afraid that the other will take too long and that there will be talk." Finally, after some negotiations, the physician agreed to give an intravenous euthanatic (pentobarbital and curare). The patient expired. "I did not sign the death certificate; this was the nursing home's death, and if they wanted to write something else, that was their problem."

Case 17 (Source F)

The patient, a 61-year-old man with lung cancer, was referred to this hospital by his family doctor because he could no longer be managed at home. He underwent one round of chemotherapy ("because the wife thought he should") but declined further therapeutic interventions. "If he had done what he really wanted, he would never had [come back] to here."

The request for euthanasia had been documented previously, both by the family doctor and the hospital chart. The physician is vague about the rest of the details of this case. [At one point, for example, the physician said the patient was a widower, then looked at the notes and remembered the wife.] It seems that the patient was in the hospital a short time before euthanasia was performed: "There was cancer everywhere; there was no solution." The patient originally wanted an oral euthanatic, then changed his mind and asked for an injection. [This, at least, is how the doctor explained a glaring discrepancy in the story.] The prosecutor was not notified.

Case 18 (Source F)

A 34-year-old man, with AIDS and in a rapidly deteriorating position, was admitted to the hospital with *pneumocystis carinii* pneumonia. His doctors at the time felt that he needed to be put on a respirator. The patient, however, was adamantly opposed to this course of action: "He wanted no machines, no more tubes." Again, the physician is unclear here about details of this case (whether he had family, for example, or precisely what other options were offered to the patient).

In view of what the physician called "the extreme emergency," the physician called another doctor on the unit and the charge nurse. The nurse said that the patient had requested euthanasia and that this had been noted on the chart. (Again, the story is confusing here—there is a discrepancy, for example, in the timing of the request for euthanasia). The physician called the hospital director, who said that no action was to be taken until the following morning. The physician presented the case to the hospital director and invited the director to speak directly with the patient. The director declined but suggested that the doctor call a chaplain: "but this is a stupid idea—this man is not religious, so what do I tell the pastor to do?" For the sake of "regularity," the chaplain spoke with the man and noted the request for euthanasia. The physician gave the patient an oral euthanatic, and the patient died within the hour. (The details of this case, and the one that follows, are difficult to judge; the physician narrating the cases seemed confused and, at times, perplexed and embarrassed by contradictions in the story.)

Case 19 (Source F)

A 79-year-old man was brought to the hospital following a stroke. A retired lawyer, he had apparently left instructions with his own attorney concerning his health care in the event he became incapacitated. Specifically, he had told his attorney that he wanted to be euthanized if he became incapacitated and unable to speak on his own behalf.

"This was a very big stroke, total [paralysis] on the one side of the body, very little response." The patient's attorney and wife apparently spoke first with the hospital director: "I am called to the director's office and shown these documents for euthanasia." The physician spoke with the wife and suggested a waiting period: "Because what does one know in these cases? I have seen worse, but this was very bad." (That is, the physician had seen worse strokes from which there had been some recovery but admitted this one was particularly severe.) The wife agreed but insisted on no aggressive therapy ("she wanted no machines") and did not want her husband transferred to a nursing facility.

The request for euthanasia was honored, although the physician is unclear on how long the patient was in the hospital ("but at least a few weeks; there was no getting better here, only worse"). The physician is clear on the patient's unresponsiveness and inability to communicate ("no signs . . . no talk . . . asleep most of the time"). Euthanasia was accomplished with phenobarbital and curare. The prosecutor was not notified.

Case 20 (Source G)

The case was narrated by a bioethicist at a large hospital who chaired the hospital's ethics committee and the terminal-care committee. The case involved a neonate, born at term, who had Down's syndrome.

"But the problem here was that there was a block in the stomach [du-odenal atresia]." The parents were apparently quite distressed: "This was a third child, and the mother kept asking how she was going to take care of this baby." The ethicist, called to speak with the parents about surgery for the child, was very specific with the parents: "I said that they did not have to approve surgery; there [were] already two problems here, and who is to know how many more would come."

(The case is confusing at this point, because it wasn't clear to me, at least from this narrative, who brought up the issue of euthanasia.) The ethicist, however, submits that "once there was a decision [not to treat], it becomes a very cruel thing to starve a baby. The mother wanted no suffering [for the child], and this I told her we could do." Again, how exactly the decision to euthanize came about is difficult to ascertain. (One should note, for example, that the case says this child died at two days, so that whatever discussions took place, they oc-curred within an extremely short time frame.) What is clearer is that the child was given large doses of benzodiazepines ("to make him more comfortable") and expired very quickly. The ethicist did not ex-pressly use the phrase "euthanasia" to describe this latter action but said that the drugs were given "just to help the child along." The pros-ecutor was not notified.

(NOTE: The interview at this point became very tense. When I kept pressing for more details on the decision-making process, the ethicist said: "Do you think, perhaps, it was better to starve this child? When the parents say 'no treatment' we cannot treat, but we do have a duty to see that no suffering takes place. This is what I told the par-ents would happen. The doctor agreed, and the child did not suffer." When I continued to press the point, the ethicist responded with an-other case "that maybe you will like less than this one.")

Case 21 (Source G)

An 84-year-old woman, with Alzheimer's disease, was brought to the hospital from a nursing facility in congestive heart failure. The woman's married daughter (and the daughter's husband) came to the hospital the same day and were referred to the bioethicist. "She said that her mother had said many times to her that she preferred death to constant illness." The ethicist called the nursing home to speak with the patient's doctor, who said that the patient had Alzheimer's and that the decision to transfer the patient to the hospital had been made when she went into heart failure. The nursing home doctor further said that this patient had, in fact, expressed a desire to die many times, but it was something that this doctor did not feel up to, especially now that the patient was demented.

"What do you do in such a case? The daughter was very devoted to the mother, but this had been happening for years. It was clear that the mother had requested help with dying but that the nursing home was not going to do such a thing." Treatment for the heart failure was stopped, but the patient continued to languish. The ethicist called a meeting of the terminal-care team and explained the situation to them. [Whether or not the nursing home doctor's notes were included in the discussions is unclear, but the ethicist did say that the patient— prior to her dementia—had requested assistance with dying.] "It was clear to everyone that this was a long[-standing] request from the patient and that the family was not forcing anything here." It was agreed that euthanasia should be performed, inasmuch as the decision not to treat had not resulted in death and the patient continued to hover between life and death ("which the doctors said could happen for a lot of time"). Euthanasia was administered, although the ethicist is unclear about the methods. The prosecutor was not notified.

(NOTE: The interview ended rather abruptly here; these were all the cases the ethicist would discuss, and according to the ethicist, there was nothing more to be added to the matter.)

Case 22 (Source H)

A 56-year-old man was brought into a hospital emergency room with massive internal injuries following a car accident. A member of the intensive-care staff [the narrator] was called to the emergency room by the surgeon on call. "The surgeon asked what was to be done here? Should there be an operation with such damage to the chest and the brain? Soon there would be family outside. There would soon be no [brain] signals for a neurologist to see; do you put the patient on a respirator?" The physician suggested that the matter end quickly: "I said, the heart will stop in some time, but if the family comes sooner, they must wait for this; it is a terrible situation." The physician, acting unilaterally, gave an injection of potassium chloride: "I think the surgeon and the nurse knew what I was going to do, but they were not there; a few minutes later, after the patient is dead, the nurse comes to ask, Is it over? I say yes, and [the nurse] comes to fix the body."

The physician did not actually consider this a case of euthanasia but of bringing on "what was surely going to happen, but perhaps after some hours." When the family arrived, they were told the patient had expired from his wounds shortly after being brought to the hospital. "In cases such as this, it is not like other cases of euthanasia; the death was at the door, and he would soon come in no matter what we did; in other cases, you know that death is near but do not know when it will come; [this latter situation] is what is euthanasia."

Case 23 (Source H)

A 70-year-old woman was brought to the hospital after a stroke by her family. "This one was very clear; the family doctor had called and said that [if recovery] was not possible, the woman had said many times that euthanasia was to happen. The family had told the same thing to me, but the words were different, saying, 'Make it easier for Mamma, do not let her sit like this forever.' Already this woman had been very sick for a long time." (The physician requested a letter from the patient's family doctor to verify the patient's request but is unclear about other details.) After "some time," it was clear the patient was "not going to be awake," and the doctor euthanized the patient but did not notify the prosecutor. (NOTE: The narrator related two other cases of euthanasia, one an 85-year-old woman with sepsis and a 55-year-old woman with colon cancer, but the stories were so confused and contradictory that they lack credibility. Further, they lack enough specifics so I felt they would not be illustrative.)

Case 24 (Source I)

(NOTE: The following interview was conducted with a group, consisting of a doctor, a nurse, and a hospital chaplain, who sat on the terminal-care team of the hospital. The three cases below were supervised by this group, but none of them actually participated in the patient's care or in performing the euthanasia.)

The patient, a 51-year-old man, had an inoperable brain tumor and had been seen, both as an inpatient and outpatient, by the hospital staff several times. During one of his visits, the patient (in the company of his wife) brought up the possibility of euthanasia. The request was referred by the attending physician to the chaplain, who went to speak with the man. After their conversation, the chaplain brought the case to the terminal-care team, who requested a psychiatric evaluation. The psychiatrist suggested the possibility of depression in the patient and recommended antidepressants and psychotherapy. The patient was started on this protocol, but there was no change in his desire to die. "We talked with him many times, as did the psychiatrist, and it was obvious that although there was depression, it was not because of a [psychiatric] illness but because of his particular situation." During a later hospitalization, the patient became more insistent ("this was one of many, many requests, and after much counseling for the family and the patient"). Feeling that the patient's request was well considered and that there was no alternative therapy for him, the team agreed to the request: "But first, we said, we have said yes, but we think you should wait some time."

The patient and the team agreed on a one-week waiting period, at the end of which he still said he wanted euthanasia. The euthanasia was performed using a standard protocol. [If the patient is able, he is given an oral euthanatic, containing barbiturates and orphenadrine in high dosages; if the patient is unable or unwilling to swallow the euthanatic himself, then the drugs are given intravenously.] In this case, the patient requested that the euthanatic be given intravenously, and he was euthanized by another physician, in the presence of his wife and a hospital chaplain. (The team went on to emphasize that their tasks include counseling and follow-up for the spouse and family in cases such as this.) The prosecutor was not notified.

Case 25 (Source I)

An 88-year-old man, well known to the hospital staff, was brought to the hospital after a "small stroke." The patient was a widower and lived with his daughter's family. On two previous occasions, the patient had requested euthanasia. He was wheelchair-bound and in failing health, and on each of the two previous hospitalizations (once for pneumonia, once for unspecified "chest pains"), he had asked to die. The hospital staff did not consider the requests serious but felt instead that they were a result of acute exacerbations of his illnesses. The terminal-care team had responded by helping arrange some support for the daughter. A visiting nurse had been contracted to come three times a week to the daughter's home to help bathe the patient and check on his medications.

On this final hospitalization, however, the patient—who recovered rather quickly from the stroke—insisted on speaking to the team himself. A representative went to take his statement, then called the hospital chaplain: "He understood exactly what the future was for him, and this was no longer tolerable. He was afraid that [after] the next [stroke], he would not be able to speak his wishes anymore, and preferred death." The daughter, informed of her father's demand, reluctantly agreed: "She had tried everything with him, but now, it was too obvious that he wanted no more help." The patient declined psychiatric intervention, and the terminal-care team, then, asked him to wait a few weeks to see if he had a change of heart.

"After maybe a few days," the patient became abusive, demanding that his wishes be carried out. A member of the team (a doctor) spoke with the patient, and reported back that no other solution to the patient's demand was apparent. The team agreed to the patient's request.

Two days later ("which were very peaceful for the patient, because he knew the suffering would soon be over"), the patient was euthanized. (The daughter declined to be involved; she had said her good-bye to her father the day before, and had asked to be called after he died.) The patient was given the euthanatic via IV. The prosecutor was not called.

Case 26 (Source I)

The case was referred by a local physician, who had been caring for an 81-year-old woman in her home who had repeatedly requested euthanasia. She was almost totally blind, had survived one heart attack, but still had severe angina. Recently, the physician had suggested to her that she needed round-the-clock care and should consider a nursing home. The woman became even more agitated and pressed her demand for euthanasia.

The family physician, for private reasons, could not accede to her demand. This doctor had called this local hospital and had spoken with the terminal-care team several times, asking for advice on the case: "We felt like we already knew this woman, her doctor had talked to us so many times." When she went into heart failure, the family physician had an ambulance take her to the hospital.

The patient's case was considered "an emergency, because we had already been told many times of her request, and here she finally was." The terminal-care team interviewed the family physician, who felt there was nothing more to be done for her but could not bring himself to euthanize her.

The patient declined counseling or psychiatric intervention; she further refused to involve "anyone else, no family or friends." The team acceded to her request, and a physician in the hospital gave the euthanatic via IV. The prosecutor was not notified.

SUMMARY CHARACTERISTICS OF THE CASES

In summary, the patients discussed in the clinical cases were evenly divided between females (thirteen) and males (thirteen). (See Table 5 for a shorter listing of the characteristics of the cases.) The average age of the women in the cases was approximately 73 years, with a range of from 28 to 89 years. The average age of the men was approximately 68 years, with a range of from 32 to 88 years. (To include the case of the 2-day-old infant changes these summary statistics to an average age of 61, and a range of from 0 to 88 years.)

Twenty-one of the twenty-six cases of euthanasia occurred in hospitals, four in the patient's home, and one in a nursing home. Twenty-one of the twenty-six cases were not reported to the prosecutor, and the bulk of those that were reported came from one source (D), a physician who worked in a hospital that required such notification.

Nine of the twenty-six patients had some form of cancer as a major underlying pathology; six had had a cerebrovascular accident (of varying severity and recentness), and one was frankly demented when she was euthanized. Four patients were described as having congestive heart failure (or being in heart failure), and two patients had AIDS. Of the remaining four patients, two had pneumonia, one was the victim of massive trauma, and one was a child born with Down's syndrome, who had duodenal atresia, which the parents declined to treat.

THE LIMITS OF THE CASES

The selection of sources, and the manner in which information was elicited, limit the conclusions one can draw from such a study. Before discussing the cases, these limitations merit further comment.

The people who narrated the cases were not randomly selected. Although their names were suggested by several sources, more than half declined to be interviewed, so there was already an element of self-selection before the interviews began. One could well theorize, therefore, that something about those who agreed to be interviewed distinguishes them from others who refused.[19] Moreover, with two

TABLE 5 Summary of Case Histories

Source Code	Patient Number	Sex	Age	Underlying Pathology	Place/Year
A-dn	1	M	67	Hepatic cancer	hospital/1985
	2	F	35	Amyotrophic lateral sclerosis	hospital/1986
	3	F	86	Pneumonia	hospital/1986
	4	F	72	Lung cancer	hospital/1987
	5	F	88	Stroke	hospital/1988
B-dn	6	M	78	Colon cancer	home/1986
	7	F	89	Stroke	home/1986
	8	F	86	Pneumonia	home/1987
C-nn	9	M	62	Lung cancer	hospital/1988
	10	F	79	Congestive heart failure	hospital/1988
D-dm	11	M	82	Stroke	hospital/1986
	12	M	32	AIDS	hospital/1987
	13	F	75	Brain cancer	hospital/1988
	14	F	28	Leukemia	hospital/1988
E-rm	15	M	59	Brain cancer	home/1987
F-dn	16	F	78	Congestive heart failure	nursing home/1985
	17	M	61	Lung cancer	hospital/1986
	18	M	34	AIDS	hospital/1986
	19	M	79	Stroke	hospital/1987
G-en	20	M	2d	Duod. atresia	hospital/1987
	21	F	84	CHF	hospital/1988
H-dn	22	M	56	Trauma	hospital/1986
	23	F	70	Stroke	hospital/1987
I-tn	24	M	51	Brain cancer	hospital/1986
	25	M	88	Stroke	hospital/1986
	26	F	81	Congestive heart failure	hospital/1988

NOTES: A capital letter in first column refers to source code; lower case letters refer to doctor (d), nurse (n), relative (r), ethicist (e), or terminal-care team (t), and whether they were speaking from memory (m) or with notes (n); duodenal atresia (duod. atresia) is the only abbreviation in the pathology category. The age of Case 20 (2d) refers to a two-day-old infant born with Down's syndrome.

exceptions (Sources B and E), the narrators of the cases were all located in the region of the Netherlands called the Ranstaad, which, in rough fashion, encompasses several urban areas (Amsterdam and Utrecht, for example) and coastal areas (Rotterdam and the Hague) and runs in a band centrally along the country to its easternmost edge. It does not include the more heavily Catholic (and conservative) southern part of the Netherlands, nor the equally conservative but Protestant northern provinces, nor the more agrarian regions of the country. Whether or not the acceptance and practice of euthanasia varies geographically (as Admiraal, for example, has suggested) is unclear, but the cases presented here are not representative of the country as a whole.

Further, all but five of the cases presented here occurred in hospitals (and one patient who was euthanized in a nursing home was under the care of a hospital doctor). Moreover, with the exception of one general practitioner (Source B) and the patient whose relative related the clinical history (Source E), the sources of information were in either university-based or tertiary-care facilities. Some have suggested that euthanasia is primarily a phenomenon that occurs in the context of family medicine.[20] Others are not so sure, noting that the attention given to euthanasia in family medicine is less a result of its prevalence among general practitioners than the lack of information on euthanasia in hospital settings.[21] In either case, I note that most of the patients discussed here died in hospitals. Whether or not this affects the details of the practice is, again, a matter of conjecture.

The reliability and consistency of the information derived from the interviews is also a matter of concern.[22] In some cases (those from Source A, for example), the physician spoke with a notebook at his or her side and referred to it during the interview. The cases were filled with details, and the narrative was smooth and fairly uninterrupted. In other instances (Source D, for example), the physician spoke from memory, and some relevant details could not be recalled. Sources H and B presented special problems. The physician referred to as Source H became confused when inconsistencies in the stories were pointed out. Although speaking with notes at hand, the physician was unable to reconcile contradictory details, and the latter two cases presented lacked credibility. Source B, as mentioned earlier, grew unhappy with the general line of questioning and cut the interview short, so I had no time to add to or corroborate details of the story. Where problems or questions arose in the narratives, I indicated as much with a note enclosed in either parentheses or brackets in the case summaries.

One could also question another source of bias in the narratives, namely, what these people chose to include or to leave out of particular stories. In other words, had these particular clinical histories been polished or edited to make them conform to what a "good" case of euthanasia should be? In at least two cases (Cases 22 and 23, Source H), I grew suspicious enough to ask the physician to repeat particular points several times (until the physician settled on one version of the story), and when a narrative appeared to change in response to a question, I made note of that. (Some omissions of detail, clearly, are a function of recall bias; in other cases, one is left with some uncertainty as to what actually occurred.) Similarly, I had no assurance that the cases picked by the discussants were not selected specifically because they conformed to an "ideal" case of euthanasia. I had originally tried to get the respondents to pick one early case, and the two most recent cases in which they had been involved. Invariably, however, people chose cases with which they felt most comfortable.[23]

Finally, there is the matter of testing and observational bias. By "testing" here I refer specifically to the way in which I asked the questions, how I reacted (perhaps inadvertently) to particular details of a story, particular lines of questioning I chose to pursue in response to the details of case, and more generally, the extent to which I was able to convey to the respondants that I could be trusted with the information they were giving me. By "observational bias," I mean the further problem of recording and interpreting the information—the extent, for example, to which I would emphasize, diminish, or ignore particular details in summarizing the cases histories.

These latter problems were of enough concern to me that I pretested the format of the interviews with one physician (who requested anonymity and whose cases are not included) in the presence of another observer who spoke fluent Dutch. At the end of the interview, I asked the doctor if there were any details about the practice of euthanasia that I had overlooked, and further asked if any of the questions or wording of the questions would seem out of place or offensive to another physician. He replied that he could not speak for others but that he thought the questions were appropriate and thorough. After the interview, I checked my version of the narratives with the interpreter, and we both agreed on the essentials of the case, though not on the relative importance of particular features of each case.[24]

What I have presented in these case histories, then, necessarily reflects to some extent particular concerns or questions I brought to the study. Nevertheless, the content of the case histories was presented to each narrator, and each was given the opportunity to correct or amend what I had heard from him or her. Thus, the histories presented were judged by their authors as essentially correct. Where the actual words of the narrator seemed important or illuminating, they are included in quotation marks as part of the case history.

What these cases say about euthanasia in the Netherlands, and what we might infer from them, are questions considered in the next two chapters.

— 4 —

From Public Theory to Private Practice: Evaluation of Case Studies

Everybody in Holland is a Calvinist. The Protestants are Calvinists, but so are the Catholics. Even atheists like me are Calvinists. And the communists here, they're the worst Calvinists of all. What does this mean? We like many rules, but we don't like to be told what the rules mean.[1]

THE EVALUATIVE CRITERIA

At first, attempting an evaluation of the practice of euthanasia in the Netherlands would seem an exercise in futility. By what criteria, for example, would one judge individual cases? There is no law directly addressing the practice, only court opinions in which it is suggested that the law will be overlooked if certain requirements are met. The government has tried, on three separate occasions, to bridge the chasm between written law and established practice, but each attempt has failed on the specifics of the legislation. Efforts to codify, for example, what is an extreme situation that compels euthanasia have failed to reconcile the opinions of those who choose to interpret the word *extreme* as implying the situation of a terminal patient in unbearable, unrelievable pain and those who believe that suffering is a matter too subjective—and therefore too private—to be dictated by public policy.

The interest of the state in protecting human life, moreover, collides in this case with the sensibilities of the medical profession in the

Netherlands, which would like a law to protect its members should they practice euthanasia but does not want a policy so detailed that it removes the element of professional judgment; nor, in fact, does the profession seem inclined to open up its practice to legal scrutiny.[2] If anything, the KNMG seems to have staked out a position far beyond the limits set by the courts and certainly in advance of actual legislation. The language of the Supreme Court in 1984, deferring in its opinion to "objective medical insight," was taken as an invitation by the profession to create criteria where none existed before. In addition, the request for guidelines from the Hague Court of Appeals, during its deliberations the following year, extended the invitation further: not "objective" medical insights, but "reasonable" medical opinion were to inform a judgment of whether a particular case of euthanasia was permissible or not.

It would be tempting, then, to evaluate the practice of euthanasia as one would any other medical practice. If euthanasia is subject to medical insight and judgment, it would seem reasonable to use established criteria that evaluate other medical practices subject to the same judgments and insights of the profession. Such a proposal, in fact, was put forward early on in the public deliberations on euthanasia by F. L. Meijler, a cardiologist at the University of Utrecht.[3] Taking note of the general sentiment that considered euthanasia a permissible practice in medicine, Meijler suggested that euthanasia be subject to the same rigorous testing and evaluation that normally accompanies the introduction of a new drug, for example, or a therapeutic technique. Specifically, his proposal would have required that every patient who died from euthanasia undergo an extensive autopsy and mortality review, one that would not only compare the physician's diagnosis with pathologies found on examination of the cadaver but would also review the deliberations leading up to euthanasia, as well as the means used to accomplish it. Meijler's proposal, which he submitted to an early commission set up by the Health Council of the Netherlands, was not accepted by any governmental or professional body, nor did it gain acceptance within the profession.

Given the demise of Meijler's idea—and this fluid state of affairs that surrounds the interpretation of guidelines on euthanasia—to suggest a rigid evaluative scheme from which to judge the current practice of euthanasia would be to create an argument that anticipates its conclusion. It seems clear, from speaking with several officials and professionals, and from the clinical histories I document, that the guidelines put forth are being variously interpreted, and in some cases, they are ignored altogether. Moreover, it also seems clear that alternative evaluative schemes—those which assume an established and clearly delineated standard of practice—would fail to capture the subtleties of this phenomenon. Standard quality assurance instruments, so much in vogue in the United States, for example, depend on not only specific and widely agreed upon definitions of acceptable practice but also the accessibility and goodwill of those being evaluated.[4] None of those assumptions holds true for the situation in the Netherlands.

What does seem a more appropriate response to the situation, however, would be to take the criteria—however loosely defined— upon which there is some consensus in the Netherlands and see how they play out in actual practice. There was no instance in which a person relating the clinical history professed ignorance of a particular guideline. Moreover, in instances in which the practice of euthanasia seemed to have gone beyond the generally assumed bounds, there was still an appeal to a more liberal interpretation of the criteria or an appeal to the exigencies of the particular case that, according to the narrator, excused him or her from following a particular guideline. Whatever the particularities of an individual patient's case, it seemed clear that the guidelines provided a backdrop against which the case evolved.

The guidelines, then, provide a generally accepted scheme within which the practice of euthanasia is to be confined. For the sake of this analysis, I restructure them according to the principles at which they aim, that is, four characteristics of a situation that, at a minimum, should be present before euthanasia can be said to have been properly administered.

The first is that a case of euthanasia be compelling: there should be unbearable suffering (either physical or psychological) on the part of the patient, and there should be no alternative measure the patient would accept that might relieve that suffering. Thus, euthanasia is to be accepted as the *ultimum refugium* only after all other options have been tried or offered, and it should occur (to use the KNMG's phrase) only when the patient and physician have "their backs to the wall."

Secondly, it needs to be established that the request for euthanasia is completely voluntary. The patient must not be acting under duress or coercion, nor under false assumptions or inadequate information; as a corollary, it is the physician's duty to assure himself or herself that this situation obtains and that the patient is exercising the right to autonomy prudently. This, at least, is how I interpret the stipulation that a patient must have a "reasonable understanding" of alternatives, a criterion that can be met only with the physician's cooperation.[5]

This interpretation of the guidelines, moreover, points to a third characteristic of permissible euthanasia: it should engage professional judgment and discretion. In other words, euthanasia is a medical act. The task of performing euthanasia may not be delegated to a non-physician, and the physician may not act unilaterally. Permissible euthanasia is to be evaluated (and executed) solely as a tool of the medical profession. Moreover, the gravity and finality of such an act dictate that the physician test his or her assessment of the situation with at least one other person. Some have chosen to interpret this latter stipulation more strictly than others, using ethics committees or terminal-care teams, for example, to evaluate a situation. Others follow a looser version of the consultation criterion, meeting only the formal requirement that one other person be involved in the decision.

However these criteria are met, they should be recorded and given some public airing. That is, the doctors need to account for their actions, at some level, in a more public forum. This fourth and final stipulation, given the data published, for example, by the Ministry of Justice, is routinely ignored in most (though not all) cases of euthanasia performed in the Netherlands and certainly in the ones I document. Nevertheless, it seems fair to include this as one evaluative element of the case analyses. The Dutch have not yet legalized the practice, and at least at a formal, juridical level, the practice is tolerated only if it can be shown that a physician's actions were careful and reasonable. Such tolerance rests, however, on the documentation and review of the particularities of a case and assumes (however disingenuously) that cases of euthanasia receive careful outside scrutiny.

In the next four sections of this chapter, then, I consider in turn how each of these general characteristics finds expression in the clinical histories of euthanasia I have documented. The related policy question of whether these guidelines, as they now stand and as they are currently enforced, sufficiently regulate the practice receives fuller treatment in my conclusion, in Chapter 5.

EUTHANASIA AS A LAST RESORT

One test of a practice's exceptional quality would be to study its prevalence, a piece of information that is clearly beyond the reach of this book, or for that matter, beyond the bounds of present knowledge. Were euthanasia a routine occurrence—were it to account, as some have alleged, for a tenth of all deaths in Holland—it would suggest that the practice had achieved rather pedestrian status, that it had become simply one more among other options available to dying patients. That euthanasia is *not* to be considered routine and ordinary care, however, is made clear by the language of the guidelines. Moreover, even if we knew the frequency of the practice, we would still be left to ponder what about these cases made them exceptional—that is, why they were excepted from the general prohibitions against killing. It has been pointed out that the reluctance of the courts or the medical profession to specify what constitutes a compelling circumstance for performing euthanasia derives, in part, from a sense that "unbearable suffering" is a uniquely personal, subjective description of one's state. It describes not only what a person feels but also how the person evaluates those sensations in relation to other aspects of his or her life and to prospects for the future. The pain or disability of young people may seem tolerable to them in light of their aspirations for the future, for example, or the loves and affections they have for the people around them, while a similar situation may be intolerable to those who see no prospects for relief and who have lost (through death, for example) the human supports that might have made such afflictions bearable. The reluctance of the guidelines to restrict euthanasia to cases of terminally ill people is in part an acknowledgment of the futility of codifying in public policy what is essentially a private judgment: once one has decided that unbearable suffering may provide grounds for justifiable euthanasia, one has all but closed the door on further qualifications.[6]

But the latitude granted by the courts on this matter is, depending on one's perspective, either the great strength or weakness of the guidelines. The range of what "unbearable suffering" means, in practice, finds wide expression in the clinical histories, and it highlights the problem of setting public limits on what is essentially private judgment. The notion of a "matter of last resort" becomes an elastic concept, stretched in various directions by circumstance.

For example, in some instances, it is an expression of the pain brought on by the lesion inflicted by the disease or in consort with the treatment for the disease. The patient in Case 1, for example, who suffered from metastatic cancer, complained not only of a persistent, cramping pain in his abdomen but also of the effects of the chemotherapy, which caused, among other things, nausea. Both the disease and the treatment for the disease caused the man's suffering. Similarly, the 72-year-old widow, who is the subject of Case 4, had already undergone surgical treatment and chemotherapy for her lung cancer, but the widening tumor made control of her symptoms difficult. She had discontinued the chemotherapy (precisely, she said, because of the treatment's harsh side effects) and was admitted for her final hospital stay because of dyspnea (difficulty breathing—a decidedly unpleasant and alarming sensation) and pain, which the drugs her family physician was using could not contain.

Physical pain from disease, or from the abrasive effects of therapies used to control disease, was a prominent feature of almost all the case histories. It was especially notable in cases involving cancer (nine out of the twenty-six), but also figured heavily in others. The woman with amyotrophic lateral sclerosis (Case 2), for example, experienced horror at her continual hunger for air and her dependence on a respirator, and expressly asked her physician not to continue the treatments ("she asked not to suffer"). Similarly, in the cases of the two men with AIDS (Cases 12 and 18), both of whom were suffering from pneumonia on their final admissions, the constricting, painful sensation of a spreading infection in the lungs, making each breath an effort, was perceived as intolerable. Even after partial remission and relief (as in Case 12), the patient's memory of the event was harsh enough for him to insist that the therapy not be repeated a second time.

These latter cases point to another prominent interpretation of the criterion of unbearable suffering, namely, that it may also include an element of weariness, of a fatigue with either the disease or the therapies that can stave off death temporarily but not cure the underlying lesion. Thus, the 86-year-old woman in Case 3, with chronic obstructive pulmonary disease and recurring bouts of pneumonia that left her successively weaker each time, was said by her doctor "to be tired" of her illness. She had said "no more of this," which at first was taken as refusal of further treatment but which she made even more specific by explicitly requesting euthanasia. Similarly, the young woman in Case 14, with leukemia, who had been in remission for one year, opted for euthanasia over further treatment or palliation. Moreover, as the story is recounted, she had made this decision in a moment of relative good health and in consultation with her husband, preferring the certain quickness of death by a lethal drug over the slower course of a natural death (and certainly over further curative interventions).

The weariness that comes from fighting a disease, moreover, can become unbearable in light of other circumstances. One could plausibly suggest that the absence of family or friends, for example, plays a role in some patients' request for euthanasia. The man in Case 1 was divorced and had no children. In six other cases, the people narrating the histories made note of the death of a spouse, the absence of children, or a situation of virtual social isolation. The 81-year-old woman in Case 26, for example, was almost blind and living alone. Although the narrative is not precise on this point, the woman's phrase that she wanted "no family, no friends" involved suggests, at the very least, some distance or estrangement in her social relations. Similarly, the narrative of the 89-year-old woman described in Case 7, alludes to a frail person disengaged from most social contacts. The efforts of her physician to relieve her burden (by enlisting the aid of a visiting nurse and part-time helper, for example) failed to mollify her desire to die. Even the physician's attempt to engage her son in the deliberations was futile. The only social contact mentioned in the narrative was a neighbor, who went with the patient to plead the sincerity of the patient's desire to die.

Under current interpretations of the guidelines, moreover, a compelling case for euthanasia can be derived from more subtle criteria. A fear of indefinite dependence—either on a machine or on other people—was a factor in several patients' stories. In the case of the 59-year-old man with the brain tumor (Case 15), whose relative related the history, one senses that the normal life of the extended family had been completely disrupted: "Like giving everyone in the family a disease of depression," the relative says. The youngest child interrupted university studies to be with the father; another child quit a job to move back home. To be sure, there is no overt hint of coercion on the family's part in this matter; on the contrary, the story, and the manner in which it was told, bespeaks a sincere devotion to the patient. However, a sense of the extent to which one's illness impinges on and disrupts the rhythm of loved ones' lives cannot but help to contribute to a sense of "unbearable suffering."

Similarly, the loss of personal autonomy, the inability to advance or articulate one's own interests, is another facet of this issue of dependency that comes light in other histories. The lawyer in Case 19, for example, anticipated the end that he feared the most. For him, what would have been intolerable was the indefinite twilight of an unconscious or semiconscious existence. So great, it seems, was this fear, that he prepared an advance directive in anticipation of just such a possibility. When he in fact suffered a massive cerebrovascular accident, his physicians waited a short while (to look for possible signs of recovery), then consented to his prior request.[7] Case 25, involving an 81-year-old man in rapidly declining health, further illustrates this notion of someone anticipating what for him or her would be an intolerable existence. Although the physician notes that the patient made a quick recovery from a "small stroke," the event was disturbing enough to the patient that he preferred death under known circumstances to what he saw as the grim uncertainty of the future: "He understood exactly what the future was for him, and this was no longer tolerable. He was afraid that [after] the next [stroke], he would not be able to speak his wishes anymore, and preferred death." This same issue comes to the fore in Case 21, involving the woman with Alzheimer's disease who went into congestive heart failure. Although the issue of consent in this instance is much murkier (as I suggest in the next section), the physician justifies the actions taken by an appeal to the patient's prior sense of what an intolerable situation would be for her.

It is worth noting here again that the Dutch have also interpreted an intolerable situation as one involving "disfigurement of the personality," a phrase that they encapsulate in their word *ontluisteren,* a rough equivalent to our own phrase *loss of dignity.* The AIDS patients, for example, whose sense of self-worth began to deteriorate in tandem with the progress of their disease; or the man in Case 11, who said in anticipation of a devastating stroke that "this was no way for a man to live," manifest the different shadings that this word can take. Loss of self-esteem, physical deterioration, loss of dignity, or in the literal translation of the word, "a condition of not being heard"—all become compelling circumstances under which euthanasia is permitted.

Finally, I note two cases where the notion of "unbearable suffering" takes on a completely different meaning. In the narrative of the 56-year-old man with massive trauma (Case 22), the physician appeals, implicitly, to relieving the suffering of the family, not the patient. It is clear that to this physician, the patient was essentially dead. Moreover, if there "would soon be no [brain] signals for a neurologist to see," the patient would be unlikely to experience pain (or any other subjective sensation of suffering). The physician calls this a "terrible situation"; that is, it is terrible for the family to have to wait for what the physician sees as sure death. So the physician dispatches the patient out of consideration for the family.

The case of the child born with Down's syndrome and duodenal atresia (Case 20) falls even further beyond the bounds of "unbearable suffering" within which euthanasia is to be constrained. The child's inevitable mental retardation had no medical cure (though many of the children born with this syndrome do respond well to other non-medical interventions); his intestinal malformation, however, did have a known, well-tested, and efficacious surgical solution. Without surgical intervention, the child would surely have died, but only after dehydration and starvation, a particularly gruesome way for a sentient human to approach death. How the alternatives of this case were presented to the parents is not clear to me, even after pressing the narrator for more details. The ethicist who presented this history notes, "I said that they did not have to approve surgery; there [were] already two problems here, and who is to know how many more would come."

Whether the possibility of euthanasia was discussed in connection with the refusal of surgical intervention remains uncertain; the ethicist adds by way of justification that "once there was a decision [not to treat], it becomes a very cruel thing to starve a baby. The mother wanted no suffering [for the child], and this I told her we could do." This phrasing of the issue at least suggests the possibility that the availability of euthanasia made a painful decision by the parents less painful. Alternatively, it could be suggested that once the parents made a decision not to treat, the ethicist's response was to try to assure the parents that the child would not suffer. The latter possibility places the locus of suffering on the patient, and thus it finds justification for euthanasia in what would otherwise be the child's lingering and disturbing passage into death through starvation.

The former possibility, however, raises the issue of whether the existence of euthanasia changes the context in which medical decisions are made. Much as it is suggested that the desire to die must emanate solely from a patient—that the experience of unbearable suffering be uniquely the patient's—the clinical histories of these patients suggest that unbearable suffering is a contingent experience. The data from the case histories suggest the different shadings of meaning that "unbearable suffering" can take on. The context in which one suffers, one's history, one's sense of the future, all shape the prism through which one filters an experience and finds it intolerable. However, if the experience of suffering is contingent, and if it is a prior and necessary condition that must exist before euthanasia is permitted, then one's decision to choose euthanasia, too, must contain at least some element of contingency. At the very least, physicians deciding whether or not to honor a request for euthanasia must satisfy themselves that patients' requests for euthanasia are not wholly contingent, that they do not arise solely out of temporary or remediable conditions. How this criterion is established is a problem to which the next section gives fuller treatment.

EUTHANASIA AS VOLUNTARY

Broadly conceived, the issue of voluntariness in euthanasia addresses two related dangers of the practice. One, clearly, is a fear that patients' requests for euthanasia do not reflect their own true wishes but the wishes of others. Patients acting under coercion—either tacit or explicit—from unsympathetic or overburdened family members, for example, are vulnerable to having their sentiments distorted or misrepresented. Two, voluntariness is also a function of knowledge and understanding: patients who choose euthanasia must be aware of the facts of their case, and must comprehend alternative solutions to their condition. Although not quite the same as coercion, choosing euthanasia out of ignorance or misunderstanding of one's situation undermines the concept of voluntariness. But voluntariness, like the earlier notion of euthanasia as *ultimum refugium*, takes on various meanings in the clinical cases.

The guidelines say specifically that a legitimate request for euthanasia may come only from the patient, but they are silent on precisely what means the physician is to use in determining that fact. In this sense, the determination of voluntariness rests with a judgment on the part of the physician or medical staff that patients' requests for euthanasia actually reflect their true sentiments. The lack of further instructions in this area finds expression in the varying ways that physicians or medical institutions determine voluntariness.

For instance, some institutions that allow physicians to practice euthanasia insist that a patient making such a request be approached alone, away from family, in the hopes of eliminating outside influences.[8] Others, however, make no such stipulation, and some, in fact, insist on family involvement with the decision.[9] Still others are as unclear on this point as are the guidelines.

The institutional checks that some facilities place on the practice at times did factor heavily into the determination of voluntariness in these cases. The cases from Source I, which involved a team consultation for each case of euthanasia, for example, show a consistent awareness of the potential for abuse in this area. The patient in Case

24 has his request noted "many, many times," and is initially referred to a psychiatrist for evaluation and treatment. In each instance, the chaplain or another member of the team notes the request for euthanasia, then discusses the issue with other members of the team. Even after psychiatric treatment fails to change the patient's mind, the team suggests counseling for the patient and his family before, finally, agreeing to the request. Another case from this source also suggests a reluctance to take an initial request for euthanasia at face value. The requests for euthanasia from the 88-year-old man in Case 25, for example, were met with skepticism and were interpreted at first as a call for assistance from an overburdened family. The patient in the final narrative in the series, Case 26, presents a more ambiguous situation. The terminal-care team considered her case "an emergency," but it went to great lengths to point out to me that they had been studying her case for some time and that "we felt like we already knew this woman, her doctor had talked to us so many times." Moreover, the patient declined their suggestions that she seek psychiatric help. It was only after speaking with her family physician, who could do nothing further for her, that the team agreed to euthanasia.

Institutional requirements also seemed to play a role in determining voluntariness in the cases narrated by Sources A and D. In Cases 1 through 5, which belong to Source A, the physician explicitly notes that the question of voluntariness is brought to a terminal-care team for consultation, though with varying degrees of regularity. In Case 2, for example, the request for euthanasia seems to emanate solely from the patient (though the physician notes that the family concurred with the decision). In the other four cases, however, it is unclear what role, if any, the referring physicians played in the request for euthanasia. The patient in Case 1, for example, requests euthanasia from the hospital doctor after he speaks in private with his own family practitioner. What transpired during this visit is unclear. In Case 4, it is the family physician who brings up the request for euthanasia with the hospital doctor. I pointed this out to the physician narrating the story, but the physician notes that the patient confirmed the choice for euthanasia several times after that. Similarly, the woman in Case 5 is transferred from her nursing home to the hospital under the pretext of a need for further observation, but, as the physician points out, "really . . . to know if the patient was a candidate for euthanasia." The physician who narrates the case is not personally involved with the patient's long-standing request for euthanasia, but this is what that doctor judges to be the situation from conversations with the nursing home director and from reading the woman's chart at the nursing home. Again, though, the physician narrating these cases specifies to acting only after the terminal-care team concurs with the physician's impression that the request is voluntary.

Similarly, the physician listed as Source D makes reference to a terminal-care team that helps to evaluate the voluntariness of patients' requests for euthanasia, but the cases here are more ambiguous. The 75-year-old woman in Case 13 makes what amounts to a contract with the hospital and undergoes one round of chemotherapy on the condition that if she is not satisfied with the results, the hospital will permit euthanasia. This unusual clinical history—which even the physician who performed the euthanasia says, "I do not understand very well"—has the physician coming in at the end of the case and performing euthanasia after the patient has declined other interventions. The physician, in a sense, executes a contract to which he or she was not an original party. Similarly, the story related in Case 11 by this same physician relies heavily on the testimony of the family and on a prior promise made by another physician. The physician believes that the desire for euthanasia is genuine, but it is worth pointing out that in these latter two cases, the original request for euthanasia comes secondhand, a detail that the physician who performs euthanasia finds sufficiently important to include in the narrative.

In other cases, the presence of institutional mechanisms to determine voluntariness seems to have little impact on the final determination of the sincerity and stability of a patient's request for euthanasia. In the cases from Source H, for example, which occurred in a hospital, no standards of consent are referred to other than the physician's own judgment (though admittedly there was a committee that sometimes considered "the more difficult situations"). The case of the man brought in to the hospital following a car accident (Case 22), permits no determination of the man's wishes. The narrative suggests that the man would never again be able to express his desires; it is equally obvious, however, that the physician did not want to wait for the family to see if, alternatively, there had been some prior discussions on the subject or if the man had executed an advance directive or had left some other instrument that might have documented his wishes.

In this physician's eyes such wishes would only have postponed what was an imminent death. The physician chose to avoid the subject altogether (and makes an implicit appeal here to compassion—the desire to spare the family any further anguish).[10] The physician also makes a claim that this is not really euthanasia, preferring to reserve that term for patients for whom medical intervention could, conceivably, extend their lives or alter the trajectory of their illness. Thus, in Case 23, the physician attempts to document the prior wishes of the patient by speaking to the family and to the patient's family doctor (requesting, at one point, a letter from the general practitioner) but says that the request for euthanasia cannot come from the patient because it was clear that the patient "was not going to be awake." The physician notes the avowed claims of the family and the family's doctor that the mother had previously requested euthanasia, makes a determination of the hopelessness of the case, and performs euthanasia.

In the case of the child with Down's syndrome and duodenal atresia (Case 20), there is no attempt to evaluate voluntariness from a patient clearly incapable of giving consent. The power of consent here devolves to the parents, who refuse further treatment for the child. I note, moreover, that it is unclear whether the parents actively consent to euthanasia in this case or whether the request for euthanasia is inferred from the mother's plea that the child not suffer any further.[11] The ethicist relating the case takes the mother's statement as a tacit plea for euthanasia.[12]

In other, noninstitutional settings, the determination of voluntariness rests even more exclusively with the physician or the physician in consultation with another person. In the three cases of euthanasia performed at home (all from Source B), the patients' desire for euthanasia finds documentation only in the physician's records. Source B was the only general practitioner I interviewed who did not consult outside parties. Furthermore, this physician became angry when I suggested that the guidelines stipulated such consultation. The response, "I know my patients better than anyone else," points to another aspect of voluntariness that the guidelines attempt to capture.

If, as I mentioned above, the guidelines address the danger of coercion in these matters, they also allude to another element of consent; that is, a decision to perform euthanasia must not only be voluntary but also be derived from a well-informed knowledge of the facts of the case. Yet the "facts" of a case rest, to a large extent, on the physician's knowledge, skill, experience, and particular habits of practice. They also rest on how a physician chooses to interpret and present to the patient the facts of a case. That is to say, if consent is also contingent on how a patient perceives the reality of his or her own situation, then that perception, necessarily, is colored by a physician's involvement.

I reiterate this point here because my interpretation is strongly disputed by others.[13] An alternative interpretation suggests that the

Dutch do not see euthanasia as a question of professional discretion. Rather, they see it as a matter of patient choice in which the physician either agrees or disagrees, either by honoring a request for euthanasia or by referring the patient to another physician not wholly opposed to the idea. It is, to use an alternative phrase, a matter of assisting in a suicide. To weigh in so heavily with the element of professional judgment, as I have done, they say, is to distort the manner in which the Dutch conceptualize the process.[14] It also betrays a furtive paternalism.

Without disputing that this may be the way the Dutch ideally conceive of the situation—nor denying that to conceptualize the question differently might be interpreted by them as a disguised form of paternalism—one can make a strong case that the Dutch have had to bow, however reluctantly, to another reality, namely, that irrespective of how much one chooses to elevate and defer to patient choice in these matters, an element of professional judgment is necessarily involved. To underscore this point, one need only refer back to the guidelines, which say that the patient "must have a reasonable understanding of his or her situation and of the possible alternatives," and that there be "no other reasonable solution apparent to improve the situation." Both of those stipulations necessarily involve professional clinical judgment. Were this not the case, the courts would not have restricted permissible euthanasia to instances in which a physician was a coagent in the act. Similarly, none of the policy guidelines envisaged by the government or others advancing this position have hinted at the acceptability of allowing someone to assist in suicide. Even those in the Netherlands who have claimed that euthanasia is not uniquely a *bioethical* problem, but problem of ethics more generally (thereby denying an important role in these decisions to physician judgment), have to include the role of medical judgment somewhere else in their calculation.[15] Moreover, every policy statement on the matter takes note of either the discord within the profession on euthanasia (suggesting that where there is disagreement, one cannot absolutely prohibit) or its quiet acceptance by some in the profession (in a somewhat ironic appeal to professional wisdom).

I stress this point again because it was an argument I brought with me to every encounter detailed in the clinical histories. It was of interest to me in an attempt not only to describe the clinical details of the practice of euthanasia but also to understand the somewhat more subtle role that clinical judgment and perception play in this matter. They are details not captured well by policy statements but are important, nevertheless, in policy formation. If a person is to choose euthanasia freely and knowingly, how does the person to whom that request is made, the physician, make this determination? If the person is to be given "reasonable alternatives," how does the clinician present those alternatives? Current policy formulations idealize the choice for euthanasia as the prudent and exclusive exercise of a patient's free will. However, if the ideal commands that only patients may choose whether to exit this life via euthanasia, the reality of the practice seems to suggest that only physicians may actually open the door and, in some instances, may describe where the door is to patients who cannot clearly see it.

The latter possibility was directed to me by Pieter Admiraal in response to a pointed query, namely, whether some physicians did not, in subtle fashion, present the option of euthanasia to patients as the most reasonable among several choices. Without implying coercion, my question hinted precisely at this question of professional influence in these matters. I noted, for example, that he had been quoted in print as having made the following statement:

> Contrary to most doctors, who will not discuss euthanasia with a patient before he asks for it, I also discuss the possibility of euthanasia with the patient, for it can be of great value and great comfort for many a patient. Not discussing euthanasia with a patient before he asks for it can cause the team to be completely taken by surprise if suddenly a patient asks for it. It may even shock the members of the team who may be disappointed or even angry about the request, which they did not anticipate.[16]

In person, Admiraal elaborated on his previous statement by suggesting that if one considered euthanasia permissible under some circumstances (which he clearly does), then *not* to broach the possibility with a patient was to deny the patient the full range of available options. In other words, pointing out to a patient *in extremis* that euthanasia was a possibility was precisely a way of giving the patient one more reasonable alternative. It was, according to Admiraal, also a measure of respect for a patient's autonomy:

> You may believe that these patients don't think about this in their minds, but when I ask them, they are not so surprised. It has occurred to them before. But you may also believe that they cannot stand this idea, but people are stronger than you think. Some say yes, but most

others say no. Remember that most people *do not* die of euthanasia. Even most of my patients do not die of euthanasia, and people say that I do this more than other doctors.[17]

I pressed Admiraal further on this point, asking whether he thought, however, that by raising the issue of euthanasia before the patient did, the doctor was making a declaration subject to serious error (and with serious consequences). That is, was not the physician stating to the patient, in more or less direct fashion, that a case was hopeless? I pointed, for example, to the notion that "hopelessness" may stand as a proxy for "quality of life" criteria, and that several studies done in the United States suggest that physicians may evaluate a patient's quality of life lower than does the patient.[18] Admiraal replied that I was demanding more certainty in this particular matter than existed anywhere else in medicine:

There is no determination of quality here, only what the patient wants. If you ask, Are mistakes made? Then certainly the answer is yes, but you should also ask, Do you take out an appendix that is healthy? or also, Does a doctor sometimes give a drug that kills the patient by mistake? Every time, the answer is yes. But in the matter of euthanasia, we are more careful than in [these other] situations, exactly because of the danger you ask [about]. When a case has no hope—no hope without a doubt—everyone knows this. Only then can euthanasia happen.

Whether or not Admiraal's attitude is shared by other doctors in the Netherlands who practice euthanasia is uncertain.[19] His comments directed me to an aspect of this practice that has not been well studied and which, frankly, my interviews failed to capture satisfactorily.

In each clinical history, I asked the narrator to give a history first, then I repeated the history to the narrator, allowing him or her to correct or amend the story. When it seemed from the narratives that a physician's influence was decisive, I went back and probed the matter more carefully. The relative narrating the history in Case 15, for example, said that after the patient returned from the hospital the last time, the physician brought up the subject of euthanasia. On further probing, the relative added: "It may seem a cruel thing, but it was the correct thing to do. [He] had asked many times for this, and now, all he could do was to wait in pain." It seems from the narrative that this wish had been expressed before by the relative and had been brought up separately by the family with the physician. As the relative relates the story, the physician's bringing up euthanasia at the end simply validated what both the patient and the family sensed.

In other cases, the way physicians describe their role is more ambiguous. Source A, for example, in Case 3, tells the patient that her condition will only deteriorate: "I had explained to her that each new bout [of pneumonia] was going to be worse." In a follow-up discussion, I asked whether such a statement was not demoralizing to a patient, to which the physician replied: "But the reality here is that she is not [going to get] better; is it kinder to lie to a patient who already has said 'no more'?" Similarly, I asked Source D about the timing of the discussion of euthanasia with the patient in Case 11. The man was recovering from a "very huge stroke," and after the patient regained the ability to communicate, the physician brought up the patient's previous request for euthanasia. To the physician, however, this seemed like the most propitious time, precisely because it was not clear how much longer the patient would be competent to make such a decision. The physician was already sure of the validity of the patient's prior request. However, not having previously been the patient's doctor, the physician wanted to hear the affirmation from the patient himself. The physician did not see this as influencing the patient's decision; that had been made. Bringing up the subject of euthanasia with the patient simply manifested the physician's caution in this area and was not (as the physician suggested I was insinuating) an attempt to push a weakened man into death.

The history recounted in Case 13, however, is perplexing. A woman enters chemotherapy but only after she receives assurances from the terminal-care team that she may have euthanasia if the treatment does not sufficiently palliate her symptoms. I asked the physician in this case (who was, admittedly, not involved in the earlier contract) whether by agreeing to this bargain, the terminal-care team was not tacitly endorsing this woman's worst fears: unrelenting pain from cancer—the anguish she had seen in her own husband's death from the same disease—was her inevitable end should the treatment fail? Again, the physician disagreed, suggesting that the availability of euthanasia gave the woman enough assurance to at least try one round of chemotherapy. Absent that assurance, the physician posits, the woman would not even have tried the more conventional treatment first.

Other cases collected in this study are even more troubling and point, I think, to the difficulty of assuring that a patient chooses euthanasia with a clear understanding of the facts of the case and of other options for treatment. The young woman with leukemia (Case 14), for example, chooses euthanasia after she relapses following her first induction. She in fact had made this decision during the period of her initial remission. However, relapses after a first round of chemotherapy are the norm in leukemia, not the exception. That she relapsed so soon after the initial remission (the history says within a year) bodes a poor long-term prognosis but does not necessarily doom the patient's chances for a second remission. The details of this case are insufficient to judge the exact course of this patient's leukemia; neither do they speak to whatever difficulty and pain she experienced during the initial phase of the illness and its treatment. Nevertheless, without trivializing this patient's suffering—and without judging *post hoc* her decision—one should question why the decision to ask for euthanasia, in one so young, came relatively early in the disease and what the physician's role was in this decision. Were other, less toxic, palliative regimens offered, for example? The therapies available to patients such as this are not limited to a choice between full-scale, cytotoxic regimens (with all their miserable side effects) and euthanasia. A middle ground, with corticosteroids and narcotics, for example, is available. It does not cure, but palliates and slows the progression of the disease. Whether or not the patient was offered this choice, or other alternative choices, is not clear. What is clear, however, is that even given the existence of alternatives, the patient was euthanized.

Similarly, the clinical history of the 79-year-old woman in Case 10 raises again the issue of a well-informed decision. The narrative says that the patient had made her wishes known that she was not to be resuscitated in the event of a cardiac arrest; moreover, she let it be known that if she became comatose, she wanted euthanasia. Neither of these events occurred, but she enters the hospital a few months later, short of breath and coughing. Diagnosed as being in congestive heart failure, she is given appropriate therapy, and her symptoms abate. Yet she begins to press her case for euthanasia, even in this period of relative stability. What alternatives were available to this woman is, again, unspecified in the narrative. Yet it is noted that the symptoms that brought her into the hospital resolved. Whether or not her condition could have found better medical management in the future is uncertain. Given her prior history and compromised health, this resolution may well have represented little more than a temporary respite, but it does suggest that her symptoms were not beyond the reach of medicine's palliative power. Whether or not this case was made to her, and whether or not it would have made a difference in her decision, are unclear from the details of the history. As in the case above of the young woman with leukemia, however, it suggests that a patient's desire for euthanasia is influenced by his or her understanding of the medical facts of the case, an understanding that is influenced to a greater or lesser degree by the physician's skill, experience, and ability to convey this information.

In neither of these last two cases could one say with certainty that a more attractive presentation of alternatives to euthanasia would have made a difference in the patient's wishes. Nevertheless, it is troubling that readily available alternatives were not chosen by the patients and that, in the face of these alternatives, the physicians acquiesced to a request for euthanasia. It raises, at least in my mind, the question of whether euthanasia as a possibility does not, in some way, already influence clinical decisions. As an example, I return to the case of the child with Down's syndrome and duodenal atresia (Case 20). Whether or not the availability of euthanasia affected the parents' decision to decline treatment in this case is unclear from the narrative. As the narrator relates the story, the parents declined treatment first, then the issue of euthanasia arose. However, the short length of time within which the decision occurred (the child was 2 days old) should give one pause.

How the clinician presented the alternatives to the parents appears nowhere in the narrative. It is the ethicist called in to consult on the case who tells the story here. The ethicist is loathe to call this a case of euthanasia, and the treatment the clinician chose in the case (large doses of benzodiazepines to make the child "more comfortable") suggests at least some ambivalence, if not in intent, then, in the resolution and rationalization of the case. Benzodiazepines are relatively safe drugs; curare is not. The ethicist, however, did agree that the drug was given in sufficient doses so that whatever agony the child felt would be palliated first, then ended, by toxic levels of the drug. The choice of medications points again to the role of clinical judgment in these cases. It points, too, to the enormous influence a physician can have in these matters.

EUTHANASIA AS A MEDICAL TOOL

Irrespective of how much one suggests that euthanasia is solely a patient-centered and patient-directed choice, one cannot escape noticing in these cases that the physician does more than simply accede to a request. Placing euthanasia in the context of medical practice subjects it to some of the same routines and habits of other medical practices. It is important, then, to see how medicine has responded professionally to this new practice.

Some may note a contradiction here. If euthanasia is to be the exception, and if it is to be administered only with one's "back to the wall," how does one speak of "habit" and "routine"? Dr. van der Meer, an emeritus professor of medicine at the Free University of Amsterdam, also takes note of this apparent contradiction: "It is sure that euthanasia is the exception, not the rule. But even these [exceptions] must have rules. This subject we did not know well, and it is better that we have some [guidelines] that we can test. . . . If it is something that only doctors can do, then it is something we can test."[20]

He gave an example. In one of the early cases of euthanasia in his hospital, "we made a big mistake: the patient does not die, and we have to send him home." In other words, whatever procedure the physicians used, they were inadequate to the task (in this case, the drugs were not given in sufficient quantities). The patient, who lost consciousness thinking he would quickly pass into death, awoke only to find himself alive. The patient demanded discharge from the hospital.[21]

Dr. van der Meer relates this story with embarrassment, but he also uses it as a cautionary tale. He adds that there are protocols now, which specify not only the circumstances under which the hospital permits euthanasia but also what drugs are to be used and in what dosages. The early practice of euthanasia, like the beginnings of any new therapy or technique, he says, fell prey to uncertainty and miscalculation. Bringing the practice to heel under established medical criteria—refining it using medical protocol and experimentation—is essential, says van der Meer, if physicians are to practice euthanasia. Having protocols does not change the "exceptionality" of the practice of euthanasia; it merely regularizes it.[22]

Admiraal, too, supports this view. If physicians have a duty to alleviate the pain of a patient's circumstance through euthanasia, then they should know when and how to do it properly.[23] To this end, he not only writes on the subject but also is often called on by local medical organizations to describe the techniques he recommends for such situations. His talk before the British Voluntary Euthanasia Society, for example, ends with a discussion of acceptable methods, appropriate dosages, and recommendations of preferred techniques.[24] Whenever possible, Admiraal suggests, patients should take the lethal drugs by mouth, under their own volition. Not only does this enhance patients' control over their own destiny, it also makes explicit what Admiraal says is at the core of the activity: assistance with suicide. For patients who are incapable or unwilling to administer the drugs to themselves, however, there are suitable alternatives, all of which involve narcotizing the patient first, then administering a lethal agent.

A plurality of cases documented in this study use Admiraal's latter alternative. (See Table 6 for a summary.) In nine cases, physicians administered a barbiturate intravenously, followed by a neuromuscular blocking agent (curare), to induce unconsciousness first, then respiratory arrest. In one instance (Case 3), the patient expired after administration of the barbiturate, making addition of curare superfluous. In six cases, the patient drank the lethal mixture prepared by the physician, which consisted of orphenadrine (an anti-Parkinsonian medication) and barbiturates. In one case, the patient was unable to swallow the substance and had to have the drugs administered intravenously. In two instances, potassium chloride was used (to induce depolarization of the heart muscle, followed by cardiac arrest). In one of these instances (Case 9), the nurse was unsure why this method was used; in the other, the physician performed euthanasia under irregular and furtive circumstances. Finally, in five cases, the drug or the route of administration is either unknown or unspecified.

The cases listed in Table 6 suggest that there now seems to be some regularity in the methods used to perform euthanasia in the Netherlands. Although Admiraal suggests having the patient self-administer the drugs, in most of the cases I document the drugs are administered by the physician. One should note, however, that these cases more heavily reflect the experience in hospitals. In the one series of cases from the family practitioner, all of the patients took the drugs by their own hands. Whether this reflects the different habits of practice or the different environments in which patients died is unclear; one could hypothesize that patients in hospitals tend to be sicker or more feeble, for example, than those cared for in their own homes. One hospital patient to whom an oral compound was offered (Case 14) was unable to swallow the drugs and had to have the drugs administered to her via an intravenous line.

In all but four of the cases the narrators specify there was some sort of consultation before performing euthanasia. In some instances, the consultation was formal, deferring judgment, for example, to an ethics committee or to a terminal-care team. In others, the hospital

TABLE 6 Summary of Methods Used to Perform Euthanasia

Patient Number	Route	Drug(s)
1	IV	Barbiturate, curare
2	IV	Barbiturate, curare
3	IV	Barbiturate
4	IV	Barbiturate, curare
5	IV	Barbiturate, curare
6	Oral	Orphenadrine, barbiturate
7	Oral	Orphenadrine, barbiturate
8	Oral	Orphenadrine, barbiturate
9	IV	Potassium chloride
10	IV	Barbiturate, curare
11	IV	Barbiturate, curare
12	Oral	Orphenadrine, barbiturate
13	Oral	Orphenadrine, barbiturate
14	IV	Barbiturate, curare
15	Unknown	Unknown
16	IV	Barbiturate, curare
17	IV	Unknown
18	Oral	Unspecified
19	IV	Barbiturate, curare
20	Unspecified	Benzodiazepines
21	Unspecified	Unspecified
22	IV	Potassium chloride
23	Unspecified	Unspecified
24	IV	Unspecified
25	IV	Unspecified
26	IV	Unspecified

physician consulted the family doctor originally providing the patient's care or requested psychiatric evaluation. The clinical histories of the family doctor cited as Source B did not include details of a consultation, and the doctor became angry when pressed on this point. On the other hand, the guidelines do not specify whom to consult, and the doctor clearly points out that either family or neighbors were involved in the decision to euthanize.[25] The other case (#22) in which there was no consultation results, one can safely assume, from the irregularity of other details of the case.

The notion that euthanasia has achieved a degree of acceptance and codification by the medical community receives some support from these cases. The practice seems to call for particular drugs, with proven efficacy, and there are protocols that guide the use and administration of those drugs. Moreover, with some notable exceptions, the cases receive varying degrees of collegial consultation. The physician (cited as Source D) who told the prosecutor to "pick a doctor" from the hospital roster because "everyone is involved" suggests, as defenders of the practice contend, that cases of euthanasia receive some degree of collegial oversight and input (though it is not possible, from these cases, to detail what the general limits of such consultations are).

EUTHANASIA AS A REGULATED PRACTICE

To note that euthanasia seems to be aired, broadly speaking, among members of the medical profession is not the same as suggesting that it is a well-regulated practice. Rigter, Borst-Eilers, and Leenen, who publicly claim as much, have to contend with the fact that most cases of euthanasia receive no external scrutiny.[26] Even if one takes their lowest estimate of 3,300 cases of euthanasia per year, the number of cases reviewed by the Ministry of Justice suggests that around 6% of cases of euthanasia are reported to the public prosecutor. Taking Rigter, Borst-Eilers, and Leenen's own higher estimates (5,000 to 10,000 cases per year) places the number of cases under external review at from 2% to 4%. In the cases I sampled, the prosecutor was notified less than 2% of the time.

What was most noteworthy, however, was the prime reason people gave for not contacting the prosecutor: every source mentioned saving the family embarrassment or additional grief. Notifying a prosecutor almost invariably involves some sort of interview with the family. To most of the people giving these clinical narratives, this was an unseemly and public intrusion on what should be a strictly private matter. The fear of personal liability—of prosecution—did not come up. In each of these instances, those relating the narrative felt that the guidelines had been well followed and that euthanasia was justified.

Dr. van der Meer, for example, suggested that to *exclude* the prosecutor from such cases was a matter of clinical judgment:

> What does it do to such a family to have the police come to the home, or to be having to answer such questions before a prosecutor? You must remember that after a patient is dead, the family is still a patient.

And [although] the family knows death [comes] truly [with certainty], there is still sadness, grief. Then is not the time for such questions.[27]

Admiraal disagrees and notes that he contacts the prosecutor with regularity in such cases. To do otherwise, he says, leaves the door open to abuses.[28] I asked Dr. van der Meer about this possibility—specifically, whether the medical profession was able to police itself adequately. Did he believe that the lack of formal oversight that currently exists is a fertile field for abuse?

> But do you know such doctors? Do you know this [for a fact]? Because if there exist such doctors, they should not be in medicine . . . they are bad not only here [that is, in regards to euthanasia], but bad in other places too. People here [in the hospital] see euthanasia, and it would soon be known of such bad cases. No, I do not think this problem exists here. Perhaps in your country.[29]

Dr. van der Meer also notes, however, that in his decades of practice, he thought that euthanasia was acceptable in "only a few cases." He thought it more instructive to tell of cases in which he had refused euthanasia:

> An old woman, very old, comes to the hospital many times. She says "now kill me," but I do not. She has pulmonia [pneumonia], and I treat this. She becomes better, then does not want to die. The family thought she should die, but the [right] to die is not to be given over [to another person]; if they cannot speak, they cannot die. But other times, perhaps I should have. A psychiatrist who was a friend has cancer. I cannot help him with medicines. He says he wants death, but I refuse: euthanasia is not an acute thing. But he leaves the hospital, and the next [day], the wife calls. He has died. I go to the home, and she says, "He died soon." A suicide? Perhaps, but whatever I did, it was not good medicine.[30]

If it seems to one that Dr. van der Meer's faith in the ability of Dutch medicine to regulate itself seems overly optimistic, it should nevertheless be noted that his perspective is shared by many in the Netherlands and abroad. Those who practice euthanasia invariably thought that it was being well policed by the profession itself. Moreover, many of those who do not practice euthanasia (for a variety of reasons) also seemed to think that it was not currently being abused, though they were less certain about prospects for the future.

Dr. Richard Fenigsen, whose opposition to this practice I have already noted, strongly dissents on all counts: "If people say to you that we would know about "bad" cases of euthanasia, then ask how this could be so. Do dead people now talk? Do doctors anywhere [inform] on their colleagues? Where are the prosecutors who would see such things?"[31] Fenigsen's point of view is supported by others, though they represent a vocal minority in the Netherlands. Dr. van der Sluis, a physician involved in organizing a hospice movement in the Netherlands, agrees with Fenigsen that the practice is being abused and that what passes for voluntary euthanasia contains elements of professional and societal coercion.[32] Others have conducted surveys in the Netherlands suggesting that elderly people generally oppose euthanasia (which, the authors add, expresses a fear of being involuntarily euthanized), and an alternative patients' rights movement, called Sanctuary, provides its members with advance directives stipulating that euthanasia not be performed on them under any circumstances.[33] Even Admiraal pointed out to me that some nursing homes now advertise publicly that they do not perform euthanasia, and one of the nursing homes I visited gave me a document that they hand out to the families of newly arrived residents, which declares that the facility does not practice euthanasia.[34]

What is one to make of this? My own sample of cases suggests that the guidelines are variously interpreted, though most fall within the broadest limits of permissible euthanasia stipulated by the KNMG. Some, clearly, did not meet the criteria. But the greatest curiosity to me was the unwillingness of most of the people with whom I spoke to criticize what seemed to be violations of one or more of the guidelines. In the abstract, everyone who practiced euthanasia could agree on the generalities: "Of course euthanasia may only be voluntary," said one physician. "How could it be otherwise? This is murder."[35] But the specifics of the cases made people more timid in their assessments. I mentioned the case of the child with Down's syndrome to another physician (who said he practiced euthanasia under the "most strict interpretation"). He said the case was "difficult," but he could not say that euthanizing the child was "totally in error." Perhaps, he said, he would not have done the euthanasia, but other people have different beliefs.[36] Even the case of the physician who killed the trauma victim with potassium chloride did not elicit a protest from this physician, who said again that such cases are "difficult." To another ethicist at another university hospital, to whom I brought this same case, the response was less ambiguous, "If you want rules, you should not do medical ethics. Society has limits, but people who live in those limits must still make decisions."[37]

If there seems to be such disagreement as to what the guidelines mean—or a reluctance to criticize other people's interpretation of the guidelines—what is the point of guidelines or, what is more, of enforcing the guidelines? William Roose's comment at the outset of this chapter ("We're all Calvinists") plays out well in the case histories. Broadly speaking, the Dutch do seem to like rules on this subject. No fewer than seven governmental or professional organizations have issued guidelines on euthanasia since 1981. At the same time, they cannot agree on precisely what the rules mean. To give one an idea of the flexibility of the situation, a widely discussed case of euthanasia in the Netherlands is illustrative.

In 1984, a physician was suspected of having involuntarily euthanized several patients at a nursing home in the Hague called Der Terp.[38] The physician was indicted on seven counts; three were brought to trial. The case was eventually thrown out of court because the evidence gathered was deemed inadmissible (the police had taken medical charts out of the nursing home without executing a proper search warrant). What is particularly perplexing about this case was the role of the KNMG, which entered the trial on the side of the physician, claiming that this was a matter for the medical disciplinary courts to handle, not the civil courts.[39] The physician escaped civil punishment but was censured by the profession and lost the license to practice for one year.[40]

Some have pointed to this case to demonstrate that involuntary euthanasia does not go unnoticed (though the physician went unpunished, it was due to a procedural technicality). Others call the case an embarrassment and say that it does not represent the status of euthanasia in the Netherlands.[41] Opponents of the practice, however, use the case to bolster their contention that, at the very least, the current practice of euthanasia merits further regulation (though they believe that any regulatory policy will fall short of what the situation would require).

HOW PUBLIC A PUBLIC POLICY?

Whether or not the Der Terp case is representative of the practice of euthanasia or an aberration is a question that cannot yet be answered. Moreover, I would further cast the same doubt on being able to generalize from the cases I gathered. Both the Der Terp case and the clinical histories presented here point to current or potential problems in the framework now employed by the Dutch to regulate euthanasia. They also raise serious questions about the degree to which the Dutch are willing to constrain private choice in an effort to protect vulnerable patients. Said differently, the current, informal regulations that govern euthanasia in the Netherlands—at least as they seem to be interpreted and enforced—suggest a greater concern with the exercise of private discretion than with public control over the practice.

Those who would challenge my assessment here have to contend with several features highlighted in this study. The most obvious is that the formal, juridical level of this regulatory scheme is routinely bypassed. It is commonly agreed that public prosecutors do not review the vast majority of euthanasia cases in the Netherlands. In my own small sample, only a fraction of the cases I collected received judicial review. The figures derived from the Ministry of Justice and other estimates of the practice, as noted earlier, put that number at between 4% and 6%, suggesting that my sample gives a reasonable estimate of the degree of legal oversight exercised in this matter.

Yet tolerance of euthanasia in the Netherlands—at least officially—rests on the supposition that the practice has an institutional, extramedical check to it, that is, that there is a *public* process regulating the practice. The language of the courts—and on this they have, to date, all been consistent—does not give permission to perform euthanasia, but it suggests instances in which physicians who practice euthanasia will be excepted from punishment. Moreover, the rulings of the court have put the onus for justifying this practice on physicians: in admitting to having practiced euthanasia, a physician admits to a crime, and it is his or her task to prove *not innocence* but mitigating circumstances. The reasoning here assumes that the court, or agents of the court (such as the public prosecutors), will have final review. However, the data I gather in this study, both the clinical narratives and data available from formal and informal sources, strongly suggest that this situation does not obtain. At least at this most formal level, then, the public policy of regulating euthanasia fails in meeting its stated objective.

What of other, less formal mechanisms? To say that a practice is not rigidly regulated is not the same as saying that it is practiced without restraint. Those who defend euthanasia in the Netherlands, even under the ambiguities of current public control, suggest that there are other checks that may be less explicit but that still provide sufficient assurance that the practice is not abused. Here, again, I have raised objections. The first is that there is insufficient information to make that determination. Neither the Dutch government nor the legal or medical professions have been able or willing to undertake the task of characterizing this practice. Neither the prevalence nor the epidemiology of euthanasia in the Netherlands has received sufficient attention. Absent this sort of basic information, more subtle problems—such as the extent to which euthanasia alters the context of clinical decision making, for example, or the ways in which it alters the relationship between patient and physician—elude our understanding. Rather than wondering *if* the practice can be controlled, the Dutch have assumed as much and are now wrestling with problems of procedure and definition.

Here they encounter another serious problem, which leads to my second objection with informal regulatory criteria: not only are they not enforced, they are probably unenforceable. The standards under which euthanasia is currently practiced are codified with an eye toward preserving the nuance of patients' particular problems, of preserving latitude in making these decisions. In other words, they are written ambiguously. Any regulatory framework that was more detailed and specific than the guidelines issued by the courts would constrain the "private space" of patient and physician. How, for example, would one find public language commensurate with the private experience of people who want to receive euthanasia? "Unbearable suffering," *ontluisteren,* and "loss of dignity" capture something of this experience, but these terms cannot give full expression to the range and variety of human suffering. When one feels it, one knows it.[42]

On this point, the people in the Netherlands who defended the current practice of euthanasia were consistent and clear. Moreover, their conversations with me seemed to reflect accurately the frustrations of earlier commissions on this very question. One should recall that the majority report of the State Commission on Euthanasia split precisely on this issue. Of those who were in favor of permitting euthanasia under certain circumstances, some wanted the practice restricted to patients who were terminal, but others found this criterion too narrow. The restriction was deleted from the final report. The courts, furthermore, have been equally loathe to constrain the scope of permissible euthanasia. The Rotterdam court's decision in 1981, one should remember, rejected the opinion of the expert medical witness who suggested that euthanasia be performed only on patients in the final stage of their illness. Medical opinion was too speculative on this point, the court said, for restrictions to rest on it.

It strains the imagination, then, to suppose that medical opinion is less speculative on matters of "unbearable suffering." This, however, is what the logic of the Rotterdam court (and of derivative rulings) seems to imply. Thus, the physician need not determine whether a patient is in the agonal stages of his or her disease; rather, the physician needs to determine whether the patient's condition and request for euthanasia place them "with their backs to the wall." Here again, I would suggest, the criteria are not easily enforced, if they are enforceable at all. For all the difficulty that exists in determining whether or not a patient is in the final decline, it is still a judgment that could be based on criteria that are more amenable to evaluation and, hence, to public regulation.[43]

All of which leaves one to doubt the extent to which regulation is actually wanted in this area. Public institutions in the Netherlands have suggested the outermost limits of the practice, but both in design *and* in enforcement, they have placed those limits farther out than one would have imagined. They have also placed responsibility for both interpreting and enforcing public policy in the hands of a relatively small group of people, namely, physicians.

Note, for example, that the guidelines established by the Rotterdam court are addressed to a medical audience, not a lay one. Only the first condition speaks to circumstances in the patient's life that might make euthanasia permissible, that is, the notion of "unbearable suffering." Even this criterion is subject to a physician's judgment.[44] Moreover, in the second through ninth items, the guidelines deal directly with a physician's interpretation and evaluation of the request. Under the current system, doctors not only determine voluntariness on the patient's part, they are also instrumental in helping form that volition.[45] The guidelines also address matters of medical technique and protocol—euthanasia is to be performed with care and without inflicting unnecessary suffering on either the patient or those around him or her.

The guidelines, then, are instructions to physicians, but they are instructions of a peculiar sort. They in essence tell physicians to behave as physicians—but in the exercise of a practice that has traditionally been forbidden to doctors. Thus, public policy's usual forbearance in matters of medical practice dissolves: if a physician performs euthanasia, the guidelines say, he or she needs to report it to legal authorities and submit to an external review. Yet the physicians in the

Netherlands with whom I spoke balk at this sort of oversight, especially by nonmedical authorities. In this respect, they are no different than their counterparts in other countries.

Their reasoning on this matter is illuminating, and it points again to the problems with regulating the practice of euthanasia. The general practitioner (Source B), for example, became infuriated at my insistently pointing out that the acts of euthanasia performed by this doctor were never reported to the prosecutor. The comment "I know my patients better than anyone else" is the cry of a physician bristling at having his or her judgment questioned. The general practitioner was the doctor on these cases, not me, and certainly not the prosecutor. This doctor was confident of having behaved with professional integrity—behaved as the guidelines suggest a good physician is to behave—and, at least according to the narrative, killed the patient only when their backs were "to the wall." To ignore the reporting requirements may undermine the whole regulatory process, but this is not the doctor's concern and makes the doctor no less a good physician.

Dr. van der Meer's objections are even more pointed. He suggests that, in the exercise of good clinical judgment, a physician may reasonably exclude public oversight in these matters, because it is detrimental to the grieving family—which, according to him, is still under the physician's care and whose grief should be protected from public eyes. Similarly, other physicians in this study who did not notify the prosecutor cited concern for the patient's family or for the patient's reputation. No one expressed a fear of being prosecuted or convicted as reason for failing to inform the prosecutor's office.

One is left, then, with this odd situation. Euthanasia has no formal legal sanction in the Netherlands, yet it finds tolerance to the extent that one can make a *public* case for extenuating circumstances. Official protestations aside, however, public regulation of euthanasia devolves, as a matter of practice, onto a particular segment of society—the physicians. Neither the courts nor the other branches of the Dutch government seem to play as active a role in managing and restricting euthanasia as the guidelines would imply, nor as defenders of the practice in the Netherlands have suggested. The role of both participant and regulator has fallen to the medical practitioners, with what seems to be the tacit consent of most of the rest of Dutch society.

I find this a deeply troubling state of affairs. If, as I have tried to demonstrate, restraint and regulation in the matter of euthanasia rests, to a large extent, on the individual practitioners, it bespeaks a remarkable trust in the medical profession in the Netherlands or an almost cavalier attitude toward those—however many or few their numbers—who cannot challenge a decision to have euthanasia performed on them. Public policy regarding euthanasia in the Netherlands operates under the assumption that the responsible parties—physicians and patients—will exercise this enormous autonomy with wisdom and caution. To the extent that public policy fails to protect those who can be neither responsible nor truly autonomous from those who are neither wise nor cautious, it fails altogether. In my concluding chapter, I raise again this issue of vulnerable patients and argue that this policy not only fails but also endangers them.

— *5* —

The Dangers of Regulating an Active Death: Summary and Conclusions

If you look at the manners of everyday life, there is no race more open to humanity and kindness or less given to wildness or ferocious behavior. It is a straightforward nature, without treachery or deceit and not prone to any serious vices . . . if there are few deeply learned scholars . . . this may be due to the luxury of life, or it may be that they think more of moral excellence than excellence in scholarship.[1]

The general framework of secular morality is best adapted to setting limits rather than to defining what is good. General philosophical reflections can more easily establish limits to the authority of others to intervene than indicate what individuals should do with the liberty that such limits secure.[2]

DYING AND THE LIMITS OF PUBLIC INTERVENTION

In Chapter 1, I posed a question I felt lacked an adequate answer: How should we die? I asked the question, nevertheless, as a way of presenting an answer that others have given to the question. Even if we cannot answer this question for others, the response goes, as a matter of public policy we should not presume that others cannot answer it for themselves. In the absence of generally agreed upon principles, a liberal democracy limits what the state may and may not regu-

127

late in the lives of its citizens. The state may prohibit or modify actions that harm others, but it is generally silent when it cannot be shown that an action damages another.

This, at least, is how I take H. Tristram Engelhardt's comment on "general secular principles," and I think it to be a fair representation of the dominant view in the Netherlands.[3] The practice of voluntary euthanasia, specifically, is taken as the case in point. The practice does not harm others, so the argument goes; it finds acceptance among a good number (perhaps an absolute majority) of its citizens, and the boundaries on the practice that have been promulgated give a tolerable degree of assurance that it will not be abused. The government of the Netherlands, its courts, its medical profession, and a good number of its policy theorists have said as much publicly. My own conversations with Dutch officials, physicians, and ethicists confirm that this is how the matter is perceived. And whatever comes in the future of the practice's political and legal fortunes, it seems to have found temporary home in Holland, under what seem to be ambiguous circumstances.

What I want to submit by way of concluding remarks challenges this view. More specifically, I want to argue from the particulars of the Dutch situation to more general observations and suggest something about the dangers of giving public sanction to this practice. Finally, I want to end with some remarks suggesting how the Dutch situation may be instructive to the current debate in the United States over the permissibility of euthanasia.

THE DUTCH AND EUTHANASIA:
MAKING THE FACTS FIT AN ARGUMENT

To begin with, the Dutch position on euthanasia—at least as it has evolved to date—is deceiving, and it is an active sort of deception. Apologists for the current status of public policy in this area suggest that the guidelines on euthanasia are crafted with an eye toward restricting the practice—that they are written, in the words of one recent commentary, so as to "narrow" permissible euthanasia.[4] In fact, however, my reading and analysis of the situation suggest precisely the opposite. Euthanasia is already formally a crime; the recent rulings of the courts, and the guidelines derived from those rulings, have narrowed not the *practice* of assisted suicide but, rather, *instances in which the practice will be prosecuted.* In other words, the evolution of guidelines on euthanasia has been expansive, not constraining.

Some will suggest here that I am pointing to the obvious, but I think it important to reemphasize that the overall trend in this matter has been not to restrict but to extend the circle of permissible practices. The progression of legal rulings on euthanasia, for example, underscores this trend. The Leeuwarden court in 1973 convicted the daughter of killing her mother but held the sentence in abeyance, then suspended it. Moreover, this famous ruling left open the possibility of acceptable euthanasia by introducing the notion of "unbearable suffering," without specifying what was meant by this phrase. The Rotterdam court in 1981 made one attempt to restrict the practice (by convicting a nonphysician of practicing euthanasia), but the thrust of its ruling was to open wider the door to euthanasia, in essence telling physicians how they could avoid the penalties of Articles 293 and 294. What the Leeuwarden court only suggested, the Rotterdam Court codified. The following year, the district court at Alkmaar acquitted a physician who had euthanized a patient, and established that a request for euthanasia could find justification under the principle of "self-determination." The court of appeals in Amsterdam reversed this ruling (but did not assign punishment) and argued that objective medical practice did not yet countenance euthanasia. But the Amsterdam court's reasoning in this matter was rejected by the Supreme Court, which criticized the lower court's decision as being too narrow. It in turn referred the case back down to the appeals court at the Hague, with the instructions that the matter be decided not according to "objective medical criteria" but by "reasonable medical insight." The Hague court, aided by the testimony of the KNMG, acquitted the physician, arguing that he acted under a "conflict of duties."

Thus, by the time the Hague court handed down its pivotal ruling, it had already been established that there were instances in which a plea for euthanasia could be considered compelling; that is, public sentiment—and public policy—had already moved to sanction the notion that "unbearable suffering," however broadly conceived, could constitute justifiable grounds for euthanasia. Moreover, the State Commission on Euthanasia, which had already issued its final report, did not restrict assistance with suicide to instances in which the patient's condition was terminal; it suggested, in fact, that there were other intolerable conditions short of the agonal stages of a disease from which a patient might justifiably seek release.

Even if, as I have argued, the "private place" created by public policy for euthanasia is spacious, those who defend the practice still claim that the boundaries of this space are well guarded, so that neither physician nor patient wanders into it unwillingly or unknowingly. Adherents of this view submit that the current regulatory framework, however informal in practice, does have its formal checks. Here again, I contend that this claim is misleading. The formal oversight for the practice rests on two mechanisms that lack regulatory force. The first is the presumed self-reporting by physicians of instances in which they practiced euthanasia. In the vast majority of cases, this simply does not occur, for the many reasons I detailed earlier in the study. What is more, it is commonly known that this does not occur. Secondly, even in instances in which the public prosecutor is notified, the courts and their agents have been loathe to prosecute or to convict. How could it be otherwise? The physician who confesses to this formal transgression also, in essence, controls the evidence. In reporting a case of euthanasia, the physician simultaneously provides grounds for exculpation.[5]

What, then, of other, less-formal checks in this system? Once more, they are less than reassuring. The physician is instructed to consult with one other person, but that person (and the person's public function and accountability) is left unspecified. Some who seek outside review, such as Drs. Admiraal and van der Meer, do so with an eye toward legal complications and not as a test of their clinical assessment.[6] Others, such as the general practitioner surveyed in my study, find this requirement intrusive and simply ignore it. It is, moreover, irrational to believe that this stipulation could provide an effective regulatory control: those being regulated are allowed to pick their regulators. Thus, at each level of oversight, moving from the most formal and public to the least, the regulatory mechanisms under which the Dutch claim to control euthanasia are faulty.

This criticism is met, in various quarters, with remarkable equanimity. Even if the formal structure of regulation is less than perfect, comes the reply, permission to perform euthanasia rests, finally, on the integrity of the medical profession. Henk Rigter, for example, submits both in public and in private that physicians find this a distasteful function, that they perform euthanasia reluctantly, after all other options have been exhausted.[7] The real check against abuse of the practice, he suggests, comes from the Dutch physicians themselves, who display anything but enthusiasm for euthanasia. Dr. van der Meer, who expressed surprise at my asking whether physicians would abuse this practice, made this same point. Similarly, the language used by the KNMG—with "their backs to the wall"—also implies that the real brake against inappropriate use of euthanasia is an internal one: it lies within the ethic of the medical profession. Leenen, whose influential legal work in this area was noted earlier, voices similar assurances: "Opponents also argue that allowing euthanasia will undermine doctors' morale. But everybody who knows how much strain euthanasia puts upon the doctor, even when he is convinced that euthanasia is the only option, will not accept this argument."[8] The physician who accedes to a request for euthanasia, according to this line of reasoning, acts more or less under duress. Pushed to the limits of his or her professional competence by the patient's persistent cry for death, the physician is forced (to take the term *force majeure* at face value) to act outside the bounds of the medical profession and kills the patient.

This argument, however, does not stand up under scrutiny. It is an odd sort of reassurance to suggest that euthanasia is both a practice outside the bounds of professional conduct and one that can be tamed by the ethics of the profession. Public policy instructs the physician to resist euthanasia (because physicians should not intentionally kill), yet it simultaneously gives physicians the license to kill. What is offered, on the one hand, as a safeguard against abuse of the practice, is taken away by giving permission to perform euthanasia.

Some will suggest, at this point, that I have made a case for greater public regulation in this matter. My criticisms of euthanasia have centered, for the most part, on the currently ambiguous and ineffective civil restraints placed on the practice. What is now needed in the Netherlands is an enforceable code that would give greater access to public scrutiny and control.[9] The problem with the present practice of euthanasia in the Netherlands is that public policy has been vainly chasing after public sentiment. Seventeen years and several court opinions after the Leeuwarden case, there is still no standard, enforceable definition of euthanasia and its permissible practice in the Netherlands, yet the practice occurs. New laws are needed.

An attempt to draft new legislation, however, is bound to run into predictable difficulties. How, for example, would these new laws regularize the practice yet answer the objections of those (such as myself) who will wonder how well the laws afford protection? The chaotic, extralegal state of affairs that now exists in the Netherlands is no historical accident. It derives, I would submit, from an unresolvable tension in the argument of those who believe that euthanasia can be a workable public policy. The courts have wanted to give greater autonomy in this matter, but have been unable (or unwilling) to dispense altogether with legal prohibitions against killing (no matter how well intentioned). They therefore bow in the direction of both principles: euthanasia is not legalized (and as such, public prohibitions against killing remain), but physicians who can demonstrate that they practiced euthanasia as an extension of the patient's right to self-determination are not punished (thus giving the principle of autonomy a decisive role in the matter).

Attempts to fuse these two claims into a single policy, however, have failed. The state commission's final report founders on this very problem. The unanimity of the commission members dissolves on precisely the question of how much autonomy is appropriate. Is euthanasia to be permitted only for terminal cases (excluding those who are handicapped but not terminal, for example, but thereby restricting the freedom of other patients)? Or is the subjective state of suffering sufficient grounds for granting euthanasia (widening, in effect, the circle of permissible claims by loosening the criteria under which a physician could assist a suicide)? The commission chose the latter course, giving greater weight to claims of autonomy, while fracturing, in the process, what fragile consensus existed among commission members at the outset of deliberations.[10]

There is, finally, the reluctance of the Dutch medical profession in this matter to submit its members to further public control. The KNMG, in many ways, has been the most vocal and least ambiguous of the parties to this debate. It has widely embraced the autonomy argument, both for physicians and for patients. It has, further, suggested that under established canons of professional conduct, physicians can claim exemption from public scrutiny, for they have a duty to protect the confidentiality of their patients. The KNMG has also argued that where abuses of medical practice occur (as in the Der Terp nursing home case), medical disciplinary courts, not civil courts, should adjudicate the matter.

My reading of the situation in the Netherlands, then, suggests that the Dutch view of euthanasia is well encapsulated by Engelhardt's gloss on "general secular principles." The development of permissible euthanasia, governmental and institutional responses, and the acceptance of the practice by both the medical profession and the lay public demonstrate that, at least in this matter, the Dutch see little room for more explicit public control. The prevailing sentiment in the Netherlands seems to be that how one should die is so private a matter, so intimately tied to one's right to self-determination, that the state's role is to be circumspect and undisruptive.

AUTONOMY AND VULNERABILITY: REVISITING PUBLIC GOODS AND PRIVATE CLAIMS

If this is in fact the case, why then the nettlesome issue of guidelines and criteria? Why have neither the courts nor Parliament yet spoken with a clear voice on the matter? Those who find my assessment harsh can point, with some justification, to the contentious and agonizing course of policy development in the Netherlands over the past seventeen years. The Dutch, it could be argued, have not trivialized this issue but, rather, have labored long and publicly over the appropriateness of euthanasia precisely because they understand its gravity.

Understanding the gravity of a problem, and responding appropriately, may be two distinct matters, however. The Dutch have been stung in the last few years by outside accounts of their practice of euthanasia. As noted earlier, the British Medical Association's recent report on euthanasia was extremely critical of the situation in the Netherlands.[11] Those with whom I spoke in the Netherlands, moreover, were at pains to point out that this has been a matter of controversy and anguish for them and that they have not reached their decisions lightly. One can agree with this sentiment and still note that on the core issues of the controversy—how to control the practice, how to keep it from being used on those who do not want it, how to provide for public accountability—the Dutch response has been, to date, inadequate.

The argument from autonomy, at least as it has evolved in public discourse, suggests that dying is a private affair. However, this argument, at least in the hands of current Dutch apologists, goes further. One's autonomy not only encompasses the right to die as one chooses, it also encompasses the right to enlist the aid of a physician.[12] This position is advanced in even bolder language by Engelhardt, who says explicitly what the Dutch only imply:

> Against any claims regarding the importance of the sanctity of life, counterclaims can be advanced regarding the sanctity of free choice. Another way of putting this is that killing cannot be shown to be a *malum in se*, at least in terms of general philosophical arguments that do not already presuppose a particular ideological or religious view-

> point. What is wrong with murder is taking another person's life without permission. *Consent cures. The competent suicide consents* [emphasis added].[13]

In different language, this event is like any other private transaction, morally neutral as long as there are competent and consenting parties to the transaction.

To suggest that what transpires between a physician and a patient, even at the hour of the patient's death, is an entirely private matter is, however, to overlook the public institutional quality of the profession of medicine. In Chapter 1, I made an effort to establish that medicine, for all its necessarily private and intimate aspects, was necessarily a public enterprise. I pointed, for example, to obvious instances in which there was some institutionalized and public accountability to the rest of society. However, the claim to a right to death at the hands of a physician is essentially a private claim on a public good.

It is a claim that I doubt can be justified. The professional and legal prohibitions against physicians killing patients have been part of that public aspect of medicine. The reasons for this prohibition have various origins and serve various purposes, and they are argued with greater elegance and precision elsewhere.[14] However, the bans on physicians killing all point, either directly or indirectly, to the vulnerability of patients. Irrespective of how highly among a hierarchy of values one wishes to elevate patient autonomy, one cannot escape the fact that the patient, by virtue of his or her disease, comes to a physician under particularly unprotected circumstances. Debilitated by illness, weary, almost always anxious or afraid, a patient is necessarily in an unequal position with respect to the physician, by virtue of both his or her illness and the physician's presumed skill and knowledge on matters medical.[15] When a patient is dying, when he or she is racked by pain to the point of "unbearable suffering," that patient, I would contend, is even more vulnerable.

This notion of patient vulnerability is not offered by way of encouraging or excusing overbearing, patronizing, or paternalistic behavior on the physician's part. Rather, it is meant to suggest that civil restrictions on what physicians may and may not do *as physicians* have had to address this reality. Moreover, acknowledging up front another person's vulnerability in the exercise of one's profession does not give license but, rather, may command greater duties and responsibilities.[16]

CONCLUSION: TO THE NETHERLANDS AND BACK

It is here, finally, that the Dutch position on euthanasia is least defensible—both as it has been conceived and certainly as it has been practiced. If, as I have suggested, the exercise of medicine is a public good, and if, again, the proper focus of medicine's concerns is those among those who are vulnerable—the sick, the dying—then a new claim that physicians assist with suicides has to be made with the certainty that it will not corrupt the profession to such an extent that physicians become an unintended danger to those who are sick but who do not want to die.

Attempts to protect vulnerable patients in the Netherlands from this practice have been, as I have suggested, halfhearted and ineffective at best. One could plausibly make an argument that of the twenty-six patients presented in this study, each was, in some fashion, vulnerable. Moreover, I have suggested that if these people were vulnerable, the regulatory mechanisms now in place are inadequate to the task of protecting them. In many instances, one could dissent from this assessment, but several of the cases leave no doubt. The child with Down's syndrome, for example, fell prey to an act of homicide disguised as medical intervention. To suggest that he would eventually have died from nontreatment does not alter the fact that he died as the intentional result of a physician's actions. The patient in the automobile wreck died under the same circumstances and with the same justification. Others would not be as worried as I am of the remaining cases. Neither they nor I will know, however, because as matters stand in the Netherlands, euthanasia is increasingly becoming a private matter between physician and patient.

The position of the Dutch on euthanasia has enormous implications—for their own people, certainly, but also for those in the United States who are watching what seems to be an inexorable march toward a public policy similar, if not identical, to that of the Dutch.[17] I noted earlier that in most debates in the United States on euthanasia, the case of the Netherlands comes up and is generally depicted in glowing terms. Engelhardt makes the following comment:

> . . . the Kingdom of the Netherlands has now moved informally to allow euthanasia on request. Significant abuses and untoward consequences are hard to document. It appears not only morally unavoidable, but practically unproblemmatic to allow competent individuals to choose their exit from this life.[18]

Even more recently, an article in the *New England Journal of Medicine,* coauthored by two prominent internists, Christine K. Cassel and Diane E. Meier, gave an equally benign view of the situation in the Netherlands:

> Opponents of physician-assisted suicide cite the risk of "slippery slope" abuses or mistakes, but a more open process might allow a higher level of public and professional accountability, resulting in the effective limitation of assisted suicide to clearly appropriate cases and enhancing public respect for physicians. In the Netherlands, for example, euthanasia is part of public policy and is circumscribed by explicit guidelines requiring a clear and repeated request from the patient that leaves no uncertainty about the patient's competence and wish to die. These guidelines require that there be severe suffering without the hope of relief; a financially and emotionally uncoerced, informed, and consistent choice by the patient; the absence of other treatment options; and second opinions from other professionals.[19]

Should it surprise us, however, that the authors go on to say that "significant abuses and untoward consequences are hard to document"? I have tried to demonstrate that, for the Dutch, this matter has become so private an affair that "significant abuses" (whatever is meant by that phrase) would likely go undetected by public authorities. Similarly, the argument by Drs. Cassel and Meier against a "slippery slope" accepts with remarkable alacrity that the guidelines promulgated by the Dutch are not only enforced but also enforceable.

What I mean to suggest here is that there seems to be an eagerness to believe the best about the Dutch situation when, in fact, it would be more appropriate to approach the matter with a healthy skepticism. Moreover, I would encourage my colleagues and others involved in this debate—irrespective of their final position on the permissibility of euthanasia—to practice some of this skepticism. It may be, finally, that my suspicions and worries about the practice of euthanasia in the Netherlands are mostly that: concern about sporadic instances of abuse or potential for abuse that are a poor reflection of reality. Nevertheless, from the material available, I have argued that the situation in the Netherlands is not so benign—and certainly not so well regulated—as its defenders have suggested. I have pointed to deficiencies in the theory of regulation and have noted how these deficiencies play themselves out in practice. I have, moreover, suggested that if euthanasia is to be allowed, a stronger case needs to be made that what I have called the public institution of medicine not be corrupted for private purposes.

Many who are now calling for decriminalization of euthanasia in this country marshal forth arguments based on compassion for the plight of patients who are dying slow, painful deaths and who, it is argued, are beyond the reach of medicine's care. The argument *against* giving the force of law to what are exceptional cases is well stated by William F. May:

> . . . proponents of active euthanasia would permit rather than require physicians to assist patients in a mercy killing by removing all legal restrictions on such acts. In my judgment, the existence of exceptional cases does not itself argue for permissive laws. It is by no means clear that we should always legally permit what, under exceptional circumstances, we may feel morally obliged to do. The moral life sometimes requires us to move out into a no-man's land where we cannot find full protection. For other reasons, the society would be ill-advised to provide that protection. For example, the ready existence of the euthanasia shortcut might tend to discourage the development of other modes of care for the suffering besides killing them. Hard cases do, indeed, on occasion, make for bad law.[20]

Moreover, it needs to be shown how physicians can be allowed to kill at some patients' requests yet also be trusted not to kill when the temptation is there—either from the seeming hopelessness of the patient's condition, pressures from the family, or financial imperatives.

I raise this issue again because I am, at heart, a skeptic on the subject. Throughout my study and analysis of the situation in the Netherlands, I have been plagued with the sense that something other than an argument from autonomy was at work. I had the sense that some felt that certain patients were better off dead, that it was a humane act to kill them. A recent development in Dutch jurisprudence suggests that I may have been closer to the mark than I originally suspected. A Dutch neurologist has admitted that in 1987 he killed a comatose patient with a lethal injection.[21] The public prosecutor in Delft announced late in 1989 that he was going to review the matter, although, according to present guidelines, the disposition seems to be clear-cut. Leenen, in reporting the case, suggests that the prosecutor wants to try this as a "test case," with the possibility that it might force a ruling from the Supreme Court.[22] Whether this will further open the practice of euthanasia in the Netherlands, or whether it will be used by the courts to draw more definitive guidelines, is, at this point, speculation.

It will be important to follow this issue to see how the respective parties in the debate will play out their roles. The physician, in order to find acquittal, will have to make some argument based on the essential benevolence of the actions performed. Similarly, it will be important to see how far the KNMG is willing to extend the principle of self-regulation in this case and whether it comes to the defense of this physician. Finally, barring some preemptive legislative action, the Supreme Court may be forced to decide how far it is willing to extend the notion of "reasonable medical insight." If this case finds excuse in the eyes of the law, or if the Supreme Court reinterprets the guidelines governing euthanasia to permit the killing of comatose patients, a different sort of argument justifying euthanasia will have to be made.

In the interim, if euthanasia in the Netherlands is, in fact, a benign, well-regulated practice, there is ample material for an alternative study to be done. In fact, I would welcome alternative evidence and interpretations and would hope that the study be undertaken by a scholar from the Netherlands. I remain open to the possibility that the practice of euthanasia may be controlled, though it stretches my imagination to see precisely how this would occur. Moreover, I remain unconvinced that under current regulations the practice is not abused. Those in the United States who point to the Netherlands as a public policy model for assistance with suicide have not, I would suggest, looked carefully enough. If the Netherlands—with its generous social services and universal health coverage—has problems controlling euthanasia, it takes little effort to imagine what would happen in the United States, with a medical system groaning under the strain of too many demands on too few resources. I leave that to the reader's imagination.

I end, finally, with a plea that those in the United States who advocate a change in the laws prohibiting euthanasia exercise more prudence and care in their advocacy. I ask them to consider not just the particularities of those for whom they feel euthanasia would be a welcome relief but also the larger, common society of all who are dying—including ourselves. Americans have been moving, with some success, toward a system of medical care—and medical jurisprudence—that is beginning to take the *care* of dying patients as seriously as it takes the finding of new cures.[23] Irony and tragedy will abound if their attention and efforts to care for these patients more humanely are dissipated and ultimately frustrated by a debate over the permissibility of physician-assisted suicide.[24] When twelve prominent physicians published an article in 1989 on the care of dying patients,[25] what received greatest attention from both the professional and lay public was the fact that ten of the twelve authors agreed that there were some circumstances under which they would be willing to assist in a patient's suicide. Lost in the furor was the fact that there were more instructive— and more constructive—arguments on caring for dying patients, solutions that are well within our means to effect and that do not include euthanasia.

Lost, too, in the recent furor over Dr. Kevorkian's "death machine" is the plight of Janet Adkins, the patient in whose suicide he assisted, and the plight of other patients like her, both in the United States and in the Netherlands. Whatever despair drove her to seek relief from Dr. Kevorkian—who is not a practicing clinician—should give us pause, especially those of us in the medical profession who oppose euthanasia, for we are, in our lazy inattention, accomplices after a fashion to that desperation. Patients trapped in the noisy solitude of Alzheimer's disease, those dying by inches with disseminated malignancies, the crippled and the lame, the wearied sick whom we cannot cure—they all deserve the same measure of care we give to those with more promising prospects. For if we fail them, Kevorkian and the experience of the Dutch will be not the odd example but the reigning paradigm.

The cries of those who die in pain and despair, amid the studied indifference of professionals whose duty it is to attend to their needs, should be heard. That their cries are gaining in intensity stands as a reproach to us. What I ask, however, is that those desperate cries for release from pain be balanced against the needs of the voiceless, who even in their silence still have a right to live.

Notes

1 _Introduction: The Limits of a Public Death_

1. From the William Y. Sprague diary; cited in Lewis O. Saum, "Death in Pre-Civil War America," in David E. Stannard, ed., _Death in America_ (Philadelphia: University of Pennsylvania Press, 1974), 31–32.
2. Some will dispute my use of the term "lucky," suggesting that a quiet, timely death is not in and of itself sufficient to qualify the individual as fortunate. It says nothing, for example, of what came before in the individual's life, what sorrows or joys entered into the living that came before the death. Without disputing the validity of those potential objections, I use the term in constrained fashion to describe the death of an individual that lacks the characteristics of the deaths I subsequently describe.
3. See, for example, Daniel Callahan, _Setting Limits_ (New York: Simon & Schuster, 1987), 40 ff., for a discussion of what one contemporary philosopher sees as a natural, unencumbered death. Without embracing the whole of Callahan's thesis, I am sympathetic to his notion that there are some deaths that strike us as less tragic and painful than others.
4. See, for example, Philippe Ariès, _Western Attitudes Toward Death from the Middle Ages to the Present_ (Baltimore: Johns Hopkins University Press, 1974); and Ariès, _The Hour of Our Death,_ trans. Helen Weaver (New York: Vintage Books, 1982). Ariès's masterly works concerning cultural responses to human death point out that the extensive use of hospitals as a place of death is a relatively recent development:

   > By a swift and imperceptible transition someone who was dying came to be treated like someone recovering from major surgery. That is why, especially in the cities, people stopped dying at home. In New York City in 1967, 75 percent of all deaths occurred in hospitals or similar institutions, as compared with 69 percent in 1955 (60 percent for the United States as a whole). The proportion of deaths in hospitals has risen steadily since then. In Paris it is common for an old man with a cardiac or pulmonary condition to be hospitalized so that he can have a painless death. It might be possible to provide the same care by hiring a visiting nurse, but home care is less well covered, if at all, by Social Security. It also imposes on the family a burden that it can no longer bear, especially when the wife works and there is no

141

child, sister, cousin, or neighbor available. (*The Hour of Our Death*, 584.)

5. This is less often true of hospices, where workers try to adjust the dying person's routine to that person's individual needs and (within limits) wishes. See, for example, Cicely Saunders, *St. Christopher's Hospice* (London: St. Christopher's Hospice, 1977).

6. The myriad ways in which a public institution may impinge on a dying person's private world were neatly summarized by the President's commission:

> Typically, patients forfeit control over what to wear, when to eat, and when to take medicines, for example. Furthermore, they almost inevitably lose substantial privacy—intimate body parts are examined, highly personal facts are written down, and someone they have never seen before may occupy the next bed. Finally, trust must be placed in strangers selected by the institution: care is given by professional experts who might well be, and who frequently are, substituted freely for one another to accommodate work schedules and institutional needs. All of these factors serve to isolate patients, rob them of their individuality, foster dependence, and diminish self-respect and self-confidence, even when illness, medication, and surgery have not already had these effects.

The President's Commission for the Study of Ethical Problems in Medicine and Biomedical and Behavioral Research, *Deciding to Forego Life-sustaining Treatment* (Washington, D.C.: Government Printing Office, 1983), 102.

7. One classic sociological account of the profession of medicine is found in Eliot Friedson, *Professional Dominance: The Social Structure of Medical Care* (New York: Atherton Press, 1970). The themes of professional self-regulation and dominance over other members of society were later picked up and expanded upon by Charles L. Bosk, *Forgive and Remember: Managing Medical Failure* (Chicago: University of Chicago Press, 1979); and Paul Starr, *The Social Transformation of American Medicine* (New York: Basic Books, 1982).

8. For example, as described by Kenneth Arrow, "Uncertainty and the Welfare Economics of Medical Care," *Economic Review* 53 (1963): 941–69; Ivan Illich, *Medical Nemesis: The Expropriation of Health* (New York: Random House, 1976); and Starr, *Social Transformation*. Although Arrow argues that American medicine is practiced in a *distorted* economic environment, free-market theories inform his analysis. Illich likens the relationship between modern physician and patient to that between exploiter and exploited. Part of Starr's thesis is that organized medicine in the United States has incorporated (in more sophisticated fashion) aspects of the European guild system, whereby a select group maintains elements of monopoly over a practice or service.

9. James F. Childress and Mark Siegler, for example, suggest several paradigmatic relationships between physician and patient in "Metaphors and Models of Doctor-Patient Relationships: Their Implications for Autonomy," *Theoretical Medicine* 5 (1984): 17–30. Some of the models (the physician and patient as mutual contractors, for example) lend themselves more easily to the organizational paradigms listed above.

10. Thus, modern writers on ethics in medicine often approach a particular moral dilemma in medicine from radically different perspectives precisely because they

do not share a common view of the role of physicians in society. Views range from accounts that stress the historical lineage of medicine as an ancient profession, with an ethic intrinsic to its proper practice, to more relativistic theories that see physicians and patients as partners who have contracted each others' services and monies for a period of time. See, for example, Leon R. Kass, "Is There a Medical Ethic? The Hippocratic Oath and the Sources of Ethical Medicine," in *Toward a More Natural Science* (New York: Free Press, 1985): 224–48, for an argument based on the idea of an intrinsic ethic; and, Robert M. Veatch, "Models for Medicine in a Revolutionary Age," *Hastings Center Report* 2 (1972): 5–7, for an example of the contractarian model.

11. Paul Starr, *Social Transformation,* 123.

12. Starr and others have pointed out, for example, that much of what passes for standard medical practice has less to do with fact and proven results than the habits and customs of the practitioners themselves. Now-discredited therapies such as prefrontal lobotomies and "electric stimulation" for a variety of maladies were at one time espoused and employed with great enthusiasm by the profession.

13. To say that death was traditionally a private matter somewhat overstates the case. Other cultural norms and institutions—the rites of the Christian church in medieval Europe, for example, or the burial rituals of other communities—clearly made dying a less than purely private matter. Nevertheless, the extent of public intrusion into the actual progress of *dying*—as opposed to the disposition of the dead—seems to be a modern phenomenon. See, for example, Ariès, *The Hour of Our Death,* 95–139; and Patricia Fernandez Kelly, "Death in a Mexican Folk Culture," in David E. Stannard, *Death in America,* 112–33, for descriptions of other cultural institutions that broke through the private world of the dying person.

14. See, for example, Michael Bertolet and Leslie Goldsmith, eds., *Hospital Liability: Law and Tactics,* 4th ed. (Chicago: Practicing Law Institute, 1980); and William J. Curran, "A Further Solution to the Malpractice Problem: Corporate Liability and Risk Management in Hospitals," *New England Journal of Medicine* 304 (15 March 1984): 704–5, for discussions of the myriad layers of regulations that govern institutional practice.

15. Steven H. Miles and Carlos F. Gomez, *Protocols for Elective Use of Life-sustaining Treatments: A Design Guide* (New York: Springer Publishing Company, 1989), 4.

16. National Conference Steering Committee, "Standards for Cardiopulmonary Resuscitation (CPR) and Emergency Cardiac Care (ECC)," *Journal of the American Medical Association* 227 (1974): 837–64. This same consensus paper, while noting "an obligation to initiate CPR in any situation where it is medically indicated," also pointed to the fact that there were situations—such as the case of an irreversibly dying patient—where initiation of CPR would be inappropriate (834).

17. President's Commission, *Deciding to Forego.*

18. Morris B. Abram and Susan M. Wolf, "Public Involvement in Medical Ethics: A Model for Government Action," *New England Journal of Medicine* 310 (8 March 1984): 627.

19. Ibid.

20. Ibid., 628.
21. This generalization, however, is tenuous. A poll conducted by the Harris organization in 1988 found that about half of the physicians polled in the United States agreed with the statement "It should be legal for physicians to comply with the wishes of dying patients who want their lives ended" by giving active euthanasia (cited in "1988 Polls of U.S. Public and Physicians Show Increases in Support for Living Wills and Patient's Right to Decide," *Concern for Dying Newsletter* 14 [Winter 1988]: 6). A recent newspaper article on euthanasia also suggests a shift in medical opinion; see Victor Cohn, "Is It Time for Mercy Killing?" *Washington Post (Health: A Weekly Journal of Medicine, Science and Society)* 15 August 1989: 12–15. See also Sidney H. Wanzer, Daniel D. Federman, S. J. Adelstein, et al., "The Physician's Responsibility Toward Hopelessly Ill Patients: A Second Look," *New England Journal of Medicine* 320 (31 March 1989): 844–49, in which ten of twelve coauthors agreed that there were some circumstances under which they might assist in a patient's suicide.
22. U.S. Congress, Office of Technology Assessment, *Policies and Guidelines for Making Decisions About Life-sustaining Treatments in Health Care Institutions* (Washington, D.C.: Government Printing Office, 1988).
23. The substance of the regulations (which some interpreted as requiring that *all* handicapped newborns be given medical treatment, irrespective of their particular medical condition, the wishes of their parents, or the medical judgment of the attending physician) found their way into law as an amendment to the Child Abuse Prevention and Treatment Act of 1984; the original regulations are found in "Non-discrimination on the Basis of Handicap: Procedures and Guidelines Relating to Health Care for Handicapped Infants," *Federal Register* 49 (12 January 1984): 622–54. Dr. Koop's attempt to institutionalize the regulations involved posting notices in hospitals, with a toll-free "hotline" number, encouraging people to report purported violations.
24. See, for example, John D. Lantos, "Baby Doe Five Years Later: Implications for Child Health," *New England Journal of Medicine* 317 (13 August 1987) 444–47; and Loretta M. Kopelman, Thomas G. Irons, and Arthur E. Kopelman, "Neonatologists Judge the 'Baby Doe' Regulations," *New England Journal of Medicine* 318 (17 March 1988) 677–83.
25. Lantos, "Baby Doe," p. 445.
26. The JCAH (now called the Joint Commission on Accreditation of Healthcare Organizations [JCAHO]) is a private, voluntary organization.
27. Others, however, felt that HCFA's reform was born of the antiregulatory sentiments so pervasive in Washington in the early 1980s. For a comprehensive review of this matter, see Committee on Nursing Home Regulations, Institute of Medicine, *Improving Quality of Care in Nursing Homes* (Washington, D.C.: National Academy Press, 1986).
28. Ibid., 4.
29. Ironically, while this document was being drafted, the JCAH (which as JCAHO currently accredits over 80% of acute-care facilities in the United States) added to their standards manual a clause mandating all accredited institutions to have an appropriate policy on "Withholding Resuscitative Services." Moreover, the JCAHO's new standards stipulate that the policy be "designed to assure that patients' rights are respected." See *Accreditation Manual for Hospitals* (Chi-

cago: Joint Commission on Accreditation of Healthcare Organizations, 1988), 27–29.

30. And thus the language of the document is more tentative and equivocal than might otherwise have been the case.

31. That fear, in part, motivated some otherwise sympathetic people to object to the "Baby Doe" rules.

32. For a well-argued essay that reviews the current legal reasoning in this area— and that argues for broadening our understanding of what constitutes a legitimate public concern in protecting human life—see David C. Blake, "State Interests in Terminating Medical Treatment," Hastings Center Report 18 (May/ June 1989): 5–13.

33. That the *profession* of medicine is a public good finds support, in slightly different language, from a number of quarters; see, for example, Bruce Jennings, Daniel Callahan, and Susan M. Wolf, "The Professions: Public Interest and Common Good," *Hastings Center Report* 17 (February 1987): 3–10. This notion of public goods and private interests is one to which I return again in my conclusion (Chapter 5).

34. A particularly graphic example of how this could occur when the presumption is to treat without regard for patient wishes is found in "Death at a New York Hospital (with Medical and Legal Commentary)," *Law, Medicine, & Health Care* 13 (1985): 267–82.

35. This fact does not necessarily excuse us as individuals—or as members of a profession—from attending to others' needs that receive insufficient protection or attention from public policy. Inadequate or absent government reimbursement for medical care to the indigent, for example, is not in my mind a sufficient excuse for a physician's failing to render that medical care. Similarly, the charge that some institutions' termination-of-treatment protocols might make vulnerable patients *more* vulnerable may not, in itself, justify dispensing with protocols altogether. It does, however, place an added professional burden on those who implement the protocols. A claim for special protection that is not fully met in public policy may, appropriately, seek satisfaction elsewhere.

36. As I elsewhere suggest, others have noted that this is not the only problematic area in allowing euthanasia, and I agree. My specific concern here, however, is to elaborate on the policy aspects of this issue.

37. See, for example, the historical accounts, written by proponents of the practice, in Derek Humphrey and Ann Wickett, *The Right to Die* (New York: Harper & Row, 1986), 33–103; James Rachels, *The End of Life: Euthanasia and Morality* (New York: Oxford University Press), 168–88; Joseph Fletcher, "The Courts and Euthanasia," *Law, Medicine, & Health Care* 15 (Winter 1987/1988): 223–30, and Fletcher, "Medical Resistance to the Right to Die," *Journal of the American Geriatrics Society* 35 (July 1987): 679–82.

38. Teresa A. Takken, "Mercy-killing in California and the Netherlands," *BioLaw* 4 (1987): 1–6.

39. "Right-to-Die Advocate Vows Repeat," *AMA News* 20 May 1988, 1.

40. The Hemlock Society, "Three States Move to Legalize Physician Aid-in-dying," *Hemlock Quarterly* 36 (July 1989): 1.

41. Anonymous, "It's Over, Debbie," *Journal of the American Medical Association* 259 (8 January 1988): 272.

42. Willard Gaylin et al., "Doctors Must Not Kill," *Journal of the American Medical Association* 259 (8 April 1988): 2139–40.

43. See, for example, Kenneth L. Vaux, "Debbie's Dying: Mercy Killing and the Good Death," *Journal of the American Medical Association* 259 (8 April 1988): 2140–41, as well as letters in this same issue from Derek Humphrey (president of the Hemlock Society) and David Thomasma (professor of medical humanities at Stritch School of Medicine, Loyola University).

44. Tamar Lewin, "Doctor Cleared of Murdering Woman with Suicide Machine," *New York Times* 14 December 1990, B8. See also "Murder Charges Dropped in Suicide Case," *Washington Post* 14 December 1990, A19.

45. See note 44 above.

46. Illich, *Medical Nemesis,* 100.

47. U.S. Congress, Office of Technology Assessment, *Life-sustaining Technologies and the Elderly* (Washington, D.C.: U.S. Government Printing Office, 1987); and "Death at a New York Hospital (with Medical and Legal Commentary)."

48. U.S. Congress, Office of Technology Assessment, Policies and Guidelines.

49. For example, American Health Care Association, "AHCA Policy Paper: Patient's Rights," *American Health Care Association Journal* 7 (1981): 55–60; American Hospital Association, "Statement on Patient's Bill of Rights," *Hospitals* 47 (1973): 41; and American Medical Association, Council on Ethical and Judicial Affairs, "Statement on Withholding or Withdrawing Life-prolonging Treatment," in *Current Opinions of the Council on Ethical and Judicial Affairs of the American Medical Association* (Chicago: American Medical Association, 1986).

50. *In re* Quinlan, 70 N.J. 10, 355 A.2d 647, *cert. denied sub nom.* Garger v. New Jersey, 429 U.S. 922 (1976); Robert M. Veatch, "Deciding Against Resuscitation: Encouraging Signs and Potential Dangers," *Journal of the American Medical Association* 253 (1985): 77–78; and, Hastings Center, *Guidelines on Termination of Life-sustaining Treatment and the Care of the Dying* (Briarcliff Manor, N.Y.: Hastings Center, 1987).

51. Right-to-Die Advocate."

52. Ibid.

53. See, for example, James Rachels, "Active and Passive Euthanasia," *New England Journal of Medicine* 292 (1975): 78–80; and, Helga Kuhse and Peter Singer, *Should the Baby Live? The Problem of Handicapped Infants* (Oxford: Oxford University Press, 1985).

54. See, for example, Yale Kamisar, "Some Non-religious Views Against Proposed 'Mercy-killing' Legislation," *Minnesota Law Review* 42 (1958): 969–1042 (reprinted in Dennis J. Horan and David Mall, eds., *Death, Dying, and Euthanasia,* [Frederick, Md.: University Publications of America, 1980], 406–80), for objections based on secular arguments; and Paul Ramsey, "The Indignity of 'Death with Dignity,' " *Hastings Center Studies* 2 (May 1974): 47–62.

55. Albert R. Jonsen, "Beyond the Physician's Reference: The Ethics of Active Euthanasia," *Western Journal of Medicine* 149 (August 1988): 195–98; see also Leon R. Kass, "Neither for Love nor Money: Why Doctors Must Not Kill," *Public Interest* 94 (Winter 1989): 25–46.

56. Leon R. Kass, "Is There a Medical Ethic? The Hippocratic Oath and the

Sources of Ethical Medicine," in *Toward a More Natural Science: Biology and Human Affairs* (New York: Free Press, 1985).

57. Ibid.

58. Richard Fenigsen, a practicing cardiologist in the Netherlands, doubts that this trust is well placed now, precisely because euthanasia is permitted under some circumstances in that country; in "Euthanasia or Crypthanasia?" (unpublished manuscript, s'Hertogenbosch, 1987).

59. Derek Humphrey, for example, has said as much in public (Midwestern Regional Meeting of the Hemlock Society, Chicago, 20 May 1989), and this is what I take to be the position of H. Tristram Engelhardt in "Suicide and the Cancer Patient," *CA—A Cancer Journal for Clinicians* 36 (March/April 1986): 105–9.

60. Humphrey, Letter to the editor, *Journal of the American Medical Association* 259 (8 April 1988): 2143.

61. Fletcher, "Medical Resistance."

62. Miles and Gomez, *Protocols*, 16–17, 21, 69–70.

63. C. E. Koop and E. R. Grant, "The Small Beginnings of Euthanasia: Examining the Erosion in Legal Prohibition Against Mercy Killing," *Notre Dame Journal of Law, Ethics, and Public Policy* 2 (1986): 585–634.

64. For a concise explication of the current legal and political standing of euthanasia in the Netherlands, see M. A. M. de Wachter, "Active Euthanasia in the Netherlands," *Journal of the American Medical Association* 262 (15 December 1989): 3316–19.

2 *Euthanasia as a Public Matter: Legal, Political, and Professional Aspects of Control*

1. Article 293 of the Netherlands Penal Code (enacted in 1886). The fine of the "fifth category" stipulated by the code reaches a maximum of 100,000 guilders (approximately $50,000 at 1990 exchange rates).

2. Article 294 of the Netherlands Penal Code. The fine of the "fourth category" stipulated by the code reaches a maximum of 25,000 guilders (approximately $12,500 at 1990 exchange rates).

3. A discussion of the "regularity" of this practice is developed more fully in Chapter 3. For the time being, it suffices to say that researchers on all sides of this issue agree that euthanasia occurs with enough frequency to merit mention as a "cause of death" in mortality statistics in the Netherlands. Figures range from 2% or less of all deaths (cited in Henk Rigter, Els Borst-Eilers, and H. J. J. Leenen, "Euthanasia Across the North Sea," *British Medical Journal* 297 [17 December 1988]: 1593–959) to 10% and above (cited in, among other sources, Richard Fenigsen, "A Case Against Dutch Euthanasia," *Hastings Center Report* [Special Supplement, January/February, 1989]: 22–30.

4. Eugene Sutorius, personal interview, Arnhem, 19 January 1989. Mr. Sutorius is an attorney and former district prosecutor, who has defended several physicians charged with homicide (under Articles 293 and 294) for practicing euthanasia.

5. My use of the term "well-established" comes from various sources, among them, Henk Rigter, Ph.D., executive director of the Health Council of the Netherlands, who has written several articles defending euthanasia as practiced in the Netherlands. In response to a question on the frequency of euthanasia in the Netherlands, for example, he said, "The range of numbers is too great, though one hears many estimates. Still, everyone knows it is well established in the Netherlands, and if a patient wishes to die because of extreme suffering, he can easily find a physician who will help him—if the patient meets the criteria" (personal interview, the Hague, 11 January 1989). Unless indicated otherwise, all interviews were conducted in English (with the help of a Dutch-English translator, who offered clarifications where appropriate). Except where the syntax became too tortured, I transcribed the interview without editing for diction.

6. Again, commentators from various camps in this debate agree that there is, in fact, widespread support for the practice. Two 1985 surveys conducted by NIPO (a public opinion research organization based in the Netherlands, and likened by several Dutch professionals to the Gallup organization in the United States) posed this question to a randomly drawn cross section of Dutch society: "Would you be in favor of revising the Penal Code to permit physicians to end the life of sick people who voluntarily requested it?" Of those responding, 76% replied affirmatively to the question. Other surveys (which used slightly different language) estimate that from 67% to 72% of the Dutch public favors such a change (see, for example, H. J. J. Leenen, "Euthanasia, Assistance to Suicide, and the Law: Developments in the Netherlands, *Health Policy* 8 (1987): 197–206.

7. "Any doctor who practices euthanasia is, technically, guilty of homicide. I always tell physicians that who call about a difficult case. The fact that acquittal or suspended sentence is most probable doesn't remove the threat of conviction. What if such a case fell in the hands of an opposed Catholic prosecutor? What if the judge were not sympathetic? It is difficult, without sympathetic judges, to defend the doctor against the force of written law" (Eugene Sutorius, personal interview).

8. The exceptions to Articles 293 and 294 that the courts have established to permit euthanasia insist on the patient being (legally) competent and (medically) capable of discernment. Nevertheless, there have been cases of legally incompetent patients (e.g., minors) requesting and receiving euthanasia. Moreover, the focus of much of the current debate in the Netherlands concerns the rights of cognitively impaired patients (e.g., the severely demented or those in a persistent vegetative state). Although members of this latter group clearly fall outside what is countenanced by the current guidelines, they are the subject of ongoing inquiries by judicial and medical authorities about the permissibility of extending the practice to them. Prof. E. Schroten, director of Centrum voor Bio-Ethiek en Gezondheidsrecht (Center for Bioethics and Health Law), University of Utrecht; personal interview, Utrecht, 11 January 1989.

9. Thus, in the absence of statutory rules that address euthanasia directly, the courts and professional medical bodies delineate aspects of particular cases that make them permissible or (less often) impermissible exceptions to the written prohibitions against killing.

10. Most Dutch commentators point to the 1973 Leeuwarden court decision (in

which a doctor was given a suspended sentence for killing her ailing mother at the mother's request) as the public beginning of the current legal and ethical debate in the Netherlands (*Nederlands Jurisprudentie* [Utrecht, 1973], 183; cited in Leenen, "Euthanasia," 200).

11. Dr. Helene Dupuis, director of Meta-Medica (a center for the study of bioethics and health policy), University of Leiden School of Medicine, personal interview, Leiden, 24 January 1989.

12. The phrase "private space" was first suggested to me before I undertook this study by Steven H. Miles, M.D., in the context of a related public policy debate: the rights of patients to withdraw from life-sustaining treatments. We later incorporated the concept in our discussions of how public policy might be shaped so as to allow physicians and patients the latitude and privacy to decide when and how to end treatments. That the same phrase should be applied in a more radical context (and one that I had not originally envisaged) was disquieting. See Steven H. Miles, M.D., and Carlos F. Gomez, *Protocols for Elective Use of Life-sustaining Treatments: A Design Guide* (New York: Springer Publishing Company, 1989).

13. Dr. Dupuis, for example, used the expression "right to privacy" to amplify on the notion of "private place." She and others have drawn parallels between the debate over euthanasia in the Netherlands and the debates of the 1970s there and in the United States over abortion: "Where does a government stop governing? Not everything can be made into laws. In some places, you have to stop writing rules and let people make their own choices . . . especially when those choices only have results [consequences] for themselves" (personal interview). It was striking to me how often other commentators in the Netherlands brought up the same analogy. Although a thorough discussion of the validity of such a comparison is beyond the scope of this study, I am forced to refer to it again in Chapter 5 because it figures prominently in current arguments of both pro- and anti-euthanasia commentators.

14. Prof. E. Schroten, personal interview.

15. "If we didn't trust our doctors, euthanasia would be intolerable." William Roose, foreign secretary of the Netherlands Society for Voluntary Euthanasia (NVVE); personal interview, Amsterdam, 26 January 1989. Roose's sentiments were echoed time and again. This theme of societal trust in the profession is one to which I return in Chapter 5.

16. *Assistance with dying* and *mercy killing,* for example, are two terms sometimes used as synonyms for euthanasia. The first term, which is more passive and sounds relatively benign, suggests less of a need for public oversight than the more active and ominous-sounding *mercy killing.*

17. For example, one knowledgeable American bioethicist (who has studied in the Netherlands and who speaks Dutch fluently) uses the terms *mercy killing, physician-assisted suicide,* and *euthanasia* all in one article reviewing the legislative developments on the practice in the Netherlands. See Teresa A. Takken, "Mercy-killing in the Netherlands and in California," *BioLaw* 2 (1987): 1–6.

18. *Euthanasie* and *zelfdoding,* for example, translate perfectly as "euthanasia" and "suicide" or ("self-killing"), respectively.

19. Health Council of the Netherlands, "Advies inzake Euthanasie," the Hague, 1981; cited in Takken, "Mercy-killing," 5.

20. Dr. Peter Admiraal, for example, who staunchly defends this practice as part of humane medicine, uses the verbs *to euthanize* and *to kill* with equal regularity, as in "when the time came, I killed Mrs. M. with barbiturates and curare." Personal interview, Delft, 16 January 1989. Dr. Admiraal says that to use other terminology obscures the essence of what actually happens. Other physicians, however, preferred to use the term *assistance with suicide* because they felt that what is central in these cases is the patient's desire to die; the physician's task, in their view, is to honor a reasonable and mature request and to provide the means for accomplishing the suicide. See Chapters 4 and 5 for further discussions.

21. Ibid.

22. "The doctor can help, but not interfere. His duty is to make sure that the patient is making a careful decision, then to help the patient carry out his wishes" (Dupuis, personal interview).

23. Dr. Admiraal notwithstanding, few of the doctors with whom I spoke had his candor when they described their own practice. Others used the term in a more hypothetical context; see, for example, the interview with Dr. van der Meer, Chapter 4.

24. See, for example, Gregory E. Pence, "Do Not Go Slowly into That Dark Night: Mercy Killing in Holland," *American Journal of Medicine* 84 (1988): 139–41; and Takken, "Mercy-killing."

25. "Admiraal may like using the term, but most of his colleagues don't. Certainly the doctors I've defended would never use this term in court. It poisons the atmosphere" (Sutorius, personal interview).

26. The term *force majeure,* little known or used in this country, is borrowed from the French and means, literally, "a greater force." It is a term of Napoleonic jurisprudence and one that the Dutch use in their own legal proceedings, especially in cases involving physicians prosecuted for practicing euthanasia. The term means something like an irresistible force (e.g., a patient's extreme and enduring pain forces the physician to do something outside normal practice). Historically, the concept of *force majeure* has been used by the Dutch courts to excuse defendants who broke the law under coercion. (Commentary from Eugene Sutorius, personal interview).

   Professor Leenen's use of the term here is confusing; he is describing a situation requiring triage of scarce medical resources (the physician's attention), as might obtain on a battlefield or after an accident of some sort. Nevertheless, this clearly does not constitute euthanasia (unless, of course, the physician actively kills those who cannot be treated).

27. H. J. J. Leenen, "Euthanasia," 198.

28. Ibid., 199.

29. Netherlands State Commission on Euthanasia, the Hague, 1985. An abridged English translation appears in *Bioethics* 1 (1987): 163–74.

30. Sutorius, personal interview.

31. Marion H. N. Driesse, H. van der Kolk, W. A. van Nunen-Forger, and E. de Marees van Swideren, *Op leven en dood* (Of life and death) (Dieren: Blok and Zonen, 1986). The chapter from which this quote was extracted was translated by Walter Lagerway in *Issues in Law and Medicine* 3 (1988): 385–97.

32. H. J. Schmidt, *Geschiedenis van het Wetboek van Strafrecht* (History of the Penal Code), vol. 2, 440; cited in Driesse et al., *Of life and death,* 387.

33. How, for example, does a "general respect for life" manifest itself if not in respecting the particular life of an individual? The commentary on these laws seems illogical and may be an attempt to rationalize the law's relative leniency in matters of suicide.

34. I am deeply indebted to Eugene Sutorius for his painstaking effort to make these distinctions and explain them to me:

> You at least have to understand some basic differences between our legal philosophy and administration and yours if [the legal situation] of euthanasia in this country is to make sense to American readers. None of your journalists makes time to understand this, and our judges look like inconsistent or foolish because they do act like American judges.

Sutorius's summary of Dutch legal custom receives further elaboration in Leenen, "Euthanasia," 199, and in Schmidt, *Penal Code,* 202–20. An excellent and insightful essay on the differences between discretionary justice in the United States and in European countries is found in Kenneth Culp Davis, *Discretionary Justice in Europe and America* (Urbana: University of Illinois Press, 1976). For a more general discussion of the peculiarities of legal systems evolving from a Roman rather than an Anglo-Saxon tradition, see Munroe Smith, *The Development of European Law* (Westport, Conn.: Hyperion Press, 1928).

35. Sutorius, personal interview.

36. Ibid.

37. Ibid.

38. Professor Schroten of the University of Utrecht, for example, phrases the situation this way:

> In writing, the Article 293 ends in a period. The law says no one may assist another in suicide, no matter what the case. Period. In reality, Article 293 these days ends in a comma: "no one may assist another in suicide, unless . . . " and then the exceptions are created. What has happened in the Netherlands is that society and the courts have put a comma in where there [used to be] a period. The problem still is that they have not put the comma in the law books. (Personal interview, Utrecht, 22 January 1989.)

39. For example, some lower courts that have construed medical exceptions to Article 293 rather tightly (and have subsequently convicted physicians for an act of euthanasia) have had their rulings overturned by higher courts for not considering other mitigating factors. See, for example, H. R. G. Feber, "De wederwaardigheden van Artikel 293 van het Wetboek van Strafrecht vanaf 1981 tot heden" (The vicissitudes of Article 293 of the Penal Code from 1981 to the present), trans., Walter Lagerwey, *Issues in Law and Medicine* 3 (Spring, 1988): 455–68, for a more detailed review of the courts' judgments.

40. Regarding her depression, the testimony of an eyewitness states that "she [the mother] did not wish to go to the dining room . . . did not want to eat . . . tossed her food around the room," and seemed melancholy, dispirited, and fatigued.

Her cerebrovascular accident can be deduced from other details of her condition: "[The patient] was partially paralyzed on one side . . . had been tied to a restraining belt and now and again sat with her tongue hanging from her mouth." Ibid., 441.

41. Ibid.

42. For reasons I discuss below, I find it curious that this case should be cited as a landmark in the development of euthanasia guidelines in the Netherlands. Nevertheless, it is mentioned in nearly every legal discussion of the topic, and it figures prominently as a precedent-setting case in subsequent legal opinions. See, for example, Feber, "Vicissitudes," 457–59; and Leenen, "Euthanasia," 200. This case was also considered pivotal by the physicians, lawyers, and ethicists whom I interviewed, including Dr. Admiraal, Dr. Fenigsen, Mr. Sutorius, Dr. Dupuis, Professor Schroten, and Mr. Rigter.

43. The facts of this case are reprinted in *Nederlands Jurisprudentie,* 1973, no. 183, District Court of Leeuwarden, 21 February 1973; trans., Walter Lagerwey, *Issues in Law and Medicine* 3 (Spring 1988): 439–42. Further corroboration and elaboration are found in Leenen, "Euthanasia," 200; and Eugene Sutorius, "A Mild Death for Paragraph 293 of the Netherlands Criminal Code?" (photocopy of a summary statement, Arnhem, 1985), 3; and Admiraal, personal interview.

44. Ibid., 439–40.

45. Because, it said, the determination of when a patient is dying or near death remains too speculative even with the best medical judgment. Ibid., 442.

46. Ibid., 441.

47. Ibid., 442.

48. This is how one physician—in favor of legalizing euthanasia—characterized the case. In fact, he uses this case to bolster his argument that it is precisely in the absence of regulations that sloppiness of this sort occurs.

49. Although several Dutch lawyers and physicians have tried to rationalize this case to me, I still find it puzzling. The court sets out a series of criteria with which there would probably be little disagreement. The principles accepted by the court have less to do with euthanasia (as it is currently defined in the Netherlands) than with cessation of futile or unwanted medical treatment. For example, the court nowhere mentions active, intentional killing in the guidelines it stipulates at the outset of the decision. Yet the facts of the case revolve precisely around an illegal and irregular instance of medical killing. Nevertheless, having found the doctor guilty of violating one or more of the guidelines, the court in essence rejects its own legal reasoning and dismisses the conviction.

50. The founding of the Netherlands Society for Voluntary Euthanasia (NVVE), for example, came on the heels of this decision.

51. Leenen, "Euthanasia," 200.

52. Sutorius, for example, agrees with Leenen's interpretation but also admits that the literal wording of the opinion does not say precisely this. The acceptance of euthanasia, he says, is to be found by "indirection." That the court did not condemn euthanasia but, rather, condemned the *methods* used by the doctor was, he says, a monumental shift in legal thinking. If the court had wanted to condemn euthanasia unambiguously, it could easily have done so. (Sutorius, personal interview.)

53. A case in 1977 before a disciplinary (medical) court in Amsterdam acquitted a physician of killing a patient by giving an overdose of barbiturates (sleeping pills) at the patient's request. Because the matter was adjudicated outside the district court system (and was not appealed by a prosecutor to a district court), it has not been counted as instrumental in the development of policy regarding euthanasia (Leenen, "Euthanasia," 201; Dr. van der Meer, emeritus professor of medicine, Free University of Amsterdam [personal interview, Amsterdam, 23 January 1989]; Sutorius, personal interview; Rigter, personal interview).

54. The content of these guidelines may be found in several places: see, for example, Takken, "Mercy-killing," 4, and Leenen, "Euthanasia," 200.

55. The opinion in which these guidelines are contained suggests that these are matters for professional medical judgment and that it is outside the court's expertise to define or dictate what it means, for example, to be in "unbearable suffering." (Schroten, personal interview; van der Meer, personal interview).

56. "The person in the Rotterdam case was not a doctor and did not consult with a medical professional. The court's penalty here is based on a question of expertise and responsibility . . . that is, it is a medical matter" (Sutorius, personal interview).

57. Admiraal, personal interview.

58. Richard Fenigsen's "Euthanasia or Crypthanasia?" contains a well-documented section detailing the public and professional reaction to the courts' decisions on euthanasia in the early 1980s. Although he remains implacably opposed to this practice, Dr. Fenigsen admits that he champions what is clearly a minority position in the Netherlands. (Personal interview.)

59. Henk Rigter, executive director of the Netherlands Health Council notes that, in one sense, the Rotterdam decision threw the question of euthanasia out of the courts: because prosecutors can choose not to prosecute cases—and because they are likely to pay close attention to contemporary court opinion—the Rotterdam court gave prosecutors a nonbinding set of exceptions to Article 293: "It [the Rotterdam court] did not say prosecute or do not prosecute . . . it said if you choose not to prosecute, this is what you should look for, because if you do prosecute, this is what we will look for" (personal interview).

60. Leenen, "Euthanasia," 200.

61. Sutorius, personal interview.

62. Leenen, "Euthanasia," 201.

63. Feber, "Vicissitudes," 456.

64. Ibid.

65. Ibid.

66. Under Dutch law, a prosecutor may still seek to overturn an acquittal by petitioning a higher court for a rehearing.

67. Roose notes that this defense had been tried before and had failed. Previous courts had been unwilling to deny the presence of "material illegality" because, "in fact, everyone knew that the doctor had intentionally killed a patient, and whether one agrees or not with the action, it is contrary to written law" (personal interview).

68. Feber, "Vicissitudes," 457.

69. Ibid.

70. Roose notes that this was an opportunity his organization eagerly sought:

> It was a perfect case for us. The physician had been extremely care-
> ful—excellent documentation, and so on—and the patient was a
> lucid, feisty woman who made clear to everyone what she wanted.
> But two different courts had heard the same case, and each had a dif-
> ferent interpretation. It gave the NVVE a way of forcing the Supreme
> Court to resolve some ambiguities. (Personal interview.)

71. Feber, "Vicissitudes," 457. Leenen and others, however, applauded the Supreme Court's decision because "it made an opening to legally acceptable euthanasia by request," though they were critical of some technical aspects of the
court's decision (Leenen, "Euthanasia," 201).

72. Had the Supreme Court accepted this doctrine, it might have ended much of the
ensuing debate. Article 293 would have become irrelevant in cases in which it
could be demonstrated that a physician was assisting a patient in the exercise of
his or her autonomy.

73. Like the term *force majeure,* defined earlier, the notion of "conflict of duties"
also plays an important role in Dutch jurisprudence. It is intended to describe a
situation in which defendants will violate one or more of their obligations, irrespective of how they act. The term is employed by the defense in such cases to
suggest that a physician who practices euthanasia is torn between violating the
literal meaning of the law (by euthanizing a patient) or violating his or her duty
to the patient (by not alleviating the patient's suffering). Thus, the defense of
"conflict of duties" and *force majeure* go hand in hand: a physician's "conflict of
duties" in cases where a suffering patient repeatedly requests euthanasia becomes a "greater force." The physician is, as it were, compelled to act—if not
necessarily against his or her wishes, then against the normal standards of
practice.

74. The phrase "beyond [his or her] control" was seen to be important enough that
it receives considerable attention in several commentaries; see Feber, "Vicissitudes," 458; Leenen, "Euthanasia," 201; Sutorius, "A Mild Death," 5.

75. Feber, "Vicissitudes," 458. The elaboration in the quote is by Lagerwey; an alternative interpretation would use the terms *force majeure* or "conflict of duties."

76. Ibid.

77. KNMG, *Medisch Contact* 42 (12 June 1986): 770–75; also quoted in Feber,
"Vicissitudes," 460.

78. Feber, 462.

79. Either by acceding to the request or, in the case of a physician objecting consci-
entiously, by helping the patient find another physician who would accede to
the request.

80. Feber, "Vicissitudes," 462.

81. There are others who dispute my interpretation of the court's decision. Sutorius,
for example, believes that the court's opinion does not depend so heavily on
professional judgment: "Most reasonable requests seem reasonable to people
. . . whether they are doctors or not" (personal interview). Margaret Battin,
professor of philosophy at the University of Utah, has also studied the Dutch
position on euthanasia and claims that my reading of the opinion—and of

Dutch reasoning in general on this matter—is exactly backward. (Personal communication, Chicago, 20 May 1989.) See Chapter 4 for further elaboration.

82. Peter Admiraal, personal interview.
83. Dr. Fenigsen—one of those who left—relates that the KNMG has about thirty thousand members and that after publication of the KNMG's position on euthanasia, approximately fifteen hundred physicians resigned and formed a separate medical professional organization. (Personal interview.)
84. Richard Fenigsen, "The Anatomy of Euthanasia" (unpublished manuscript, 1988).
85. KNMG, "Standpunt inzake euthanasie" (Standpoint on euthanasia), *Medisch Contact* 31 (3 August 1984): 990–98. An abridged version of the KNMG guidelines appears in KNMG, "Guidelines for Euthanasia," trans., Walter Lagerwey, *Issues in Law and Medicine* 3 (Spring 1988): 429–37.
86. KNMG, "Guidelines," 430. Part of the motivation behind the KNMG's publication of these guidelines was to respond to the complaints of nurses, who felt that they were being involved, *ad hoc,* in a practice over which they had little control and for which there were no protocols.
87. Ibid.
88. Ibid. In its later opinion to the Appeals Court of the Hague, the KNMG would use the more vivid phrase "with their backs to the wall" to describe the position of a physician who accedes to a request for euthanasia.
89. Again, the KNMG's early restriction of the practice solely to physicians was intended to address the concerns of nurses, some of whom felt that written orders they were being asked to carry out were tantamount to euthanasia.
90. KNMG, "Standpunt," 990.
91. KNMG, "Guidelines," 432.
92. The KNMG does not actually use this language in the document, but in discussing the guidelines with Dutch physicians, this is the interpretation clinicians seem to derive from the wording.
93. Ibid., 432. I was witness to an example of this particular guideline in practice. Pieter Admiraal, while being interviewed in his office, refused a request for euthanasia that came from the patient of a nearby family doctor. It seemed that one of the physician's patients, a woman in her late twenties living with her parents, was dying of leukemia. The patient was a lesbian and had wanted her lover to move in with her during the final stages of her illness. The parents refused their daughter's request. The daughter, in turn, asked the family physician to euthanize her. Admiraal consulted with the physician (who wanted Admiraal to perform the euthanasia), then refused the request because "this was not a mature request. The daughter is angry at the parents, not at her illness." Admiraal suggested to the physician that he try to work out the family dilemma, then call back if he still felt that the daughter truly wanted euthanasia.
94. One should note, however, that in other statements the KNMG has suggested instances and criteria under which euthanasia might be acceptable for minors and others incapable of freely giving consent.
95. KNMG, "Guidelines," 432.
96. The translations of "death with dignity" and "tarnishing of personality" do not quite do justice to the word most often used by the Dutch in this connection, *ontluisteren. Luisteren* is the participle for "to listen"; the *ont-* prefix is priva-

tive. Loosely translated, a person who is *ontluisteren* is "one not listened to," that is, one not regarded, one who is less than human. Thus, the Dutch also use the word in describing the attributes of personhood that distinguish a human from other animals. To be *ontluisteren* is, in this circumstance, to have lost the very characteristic that makes one human. (I am indebted to Theo Boer, a doctoral candidate in theology at the University of Utrecht, for having elaborated on this definition.)

97. The guidelines end, for example, with the instruction that "In consultation with the patient, the right of the patient to secrecy shall be the point of departure for the doctor in involving medical and nursing personnel" (KNMG, "Guidelines," 433).

98. KNMG, "Standpunt," 996.

99. Ibid.

100. One former official of the KNMG, who requested anonymity, disputes my distinction here and notes that if the public prosecutor is notified, it little matters precisely what wording is used on a death certificate. In response, however, I noted that some prosecutors are more sympathetic than others to the practice and that in the absence of written documentation (i.e., a death certificate accurately filled out) informal arrangements between doctors and prosecutors could lead to more or less restrictive application of the law. I return to this point in Chapter 4.

101. KNMG, "Standpunt," 996.

102. Ibid. Whether or not such a claim would stand up in a Dutch court is debatable. Sutorius, who has defended several physicians, is convinced that such an appeal to professional confidentiality would not be accepted: "The KNMG can say one thing, but what the judge says stands. It is too risky to try such a defense . . . we already give physicians much discretion in this matter, but this may be going too far" (personal interview). Nevertheless, the wording of the KNMG seems an invitation for physicians to practice euthanasia bound only by their profession's own code and not under the scrutiny of the courts.

103. Technically speaking, the KNMG's statement does not explicitly condone euthanasia. In fact, it states at the outset that it refuses, as a corporate body, to either condemn or condone the practice but realizes that euthanasia is being practiced and wants to give physicians so inclined some guidance. On the other hand, such a disclaimer seems disingenuous. The establishment of guidelines—guidelines that could subsequently be used as a defense in court—is a *de facto* form of acceptance.

104. William A. Roose, "Law and Politics in Holland" (photocopy statement in English, published by the NVVE, Amsterdam, 1988).

105. Sutorius, "A Mild Death," 7.

106. NVVE, "Fact Sheet on Euthanasia," (photocopy statement issued by the NVVE, Amsterdam, 1988); Phillípe Schepens, "Euthanasia: Our Own Future?" *Issues in Law and Medicine* 3 (Spring 1988): 374; Rigter, Borst-Eilers, and Leenen, "Euthanasia," 1593.

107. Feber, "Vicissitudes," 464–65. The distinction between "legalization" and "decriminalization" figures prominently in the parliamentary debates that surrounded this bill. The trend of the courts had been to find *exceptions* to Article 293, not to abrogate it altogether. This legislative initiative sought to bypass the

earlier prohibitions in part by creating, in essence, a positive right to seek one's own death at the hands of another (namely, a physician) under certain circumstances.

108. The bill actually never reached the floor of the lower house of Parliament for debate. Under the Dutch constitution, all bills must be submitted to the Council of State for approval prior to parliamentary consideration. The Council of State, whose president is the monarch, consists of seventy members "of proven wisdom and judgment," who are appointed for life. In the case of the Wessel-Tuinstra bill, the Council of State found that parliamentary action would be "premature" because the state commission that was formed to consider this very matter had not yet issued its report. (Ministry of Foreign Affairs, Foreign Information Service, *The Netherlands in Brief* [the Hague, 1987], 8, 10; and Driesse et al., *Of life and death,* 385).

109. Rapport Staatcommissie Euthanasie (Report of the State Commission on Euthanasia), submitted to the queen on 9 July 1985 (published 19 August 1985, the Hague). An abridged version in English appears in "Final Report of the Netherlands State Commission on Euthanasia: An English Summary," *Bioethics* 1 (1987): 163–74.

110. The other two sections contained a comparative legal study of the laws prohibiting euthanasia in other European countries and a transcript of the commission's hearings.

111. Agreeing with earlier professional and judicial pronouncements, the commission went to great lengths to distinguish euthanasia from cessation of unwanted or futile treatment and further suggested that these latter practices fell wholly within the bounds of established and well-described medical practice (Sutorius, "A Mild Death," 11).

112. Namely, that it involve voluntary patients, capable of giving consent, and that it be practiced only by physicians.

113. The language here is similar, but not identical, to the earlier KNMG phrase "with his back to the wall."

114. Sutorius, "A Mild Death," 11. This addendum was, in fact, a tacit dissent from the Supreme Court's acceptance of "psychological suffering" as sufficient grounds for acceding to a request for euthanasia.

115. Schepens, "Euthanasia," 375.

116. This latter point, which is missing in all previously published English-language articles on the subject, was first brought to my attention by Dr. Fenigsen, who suggests that involuntary euthanasia may be practiced as frequently as voluntary euthanasia in the Netherlands. (Fenigsen, "Crypthanasia," 8–10, 56–72). See also Feber, "Vicissitudes," 464; and Sutorius, "A Mild Death," 12–13.

117. Schroten, personal interview.

118. Sutorius, "A Mild Death," 13.

119. One well-placed source, who requested anonymity on this particular point, rationalized the commission's reasoning this way:

> If it's allowable for conscious patients, if it is considered humane and suitable for them, should we not, with great care, allow it for others who cannot request for themselves? I do not mean to suggest that every unconscious patient be given euthanasia, but all you have to do is to walk into a *verpleeghuis* (a nursing home) and you see row on

row of people with tubes, with eyes closed, so [that you have to] get very close to make sure that they are [still] breathing. And you ask this nurse, "But how long has the patient been this way?" and the nurse says "Now for months" sometimes not months but years! And you have to ask, "But is it humane to allow such suffering?" (Personal interview, anonymity requested.)

This position, though more emphatically stated than most, was not isolated, and I return again to this theme in Chapters 4 and 5.

120. Brief van de Ministers can Justitie en van Welzijn, Volksgezondheid en Cultuur (Letter of the Ministers of Justice and of Well-being, Public Health, and Culture), *Proceedings of the Lower House of the States-General (Parliament)*, 1985–1986 session (sec. 19359), no. 2, cited in Schepens, "Euthanasia," 375; see also Driesse et al., *Of life and death*, 395. I should note that there is a discrepancy in reporting the contents of the ministers' letter. Schepens suggests that the ministers unreservedly supported the bill outlined in their letter; Driesse et al., on the other hand, state that the bill was sent with reservations from the ministers. Feber ("Vicissitudes," 464) is silent on the ministers' attitude but notes that the letter outlines a number of "carefulness protocols" that the lower house should consider in drafting legislation. Others queried on this discrepancy could not recall what, if any, reservations the ministers might have included.

121. Feber, "Vicissitudes," 465. One should note that the language of the Wessel-Tuinstra bill more faithfully followed the commission's recommendations. Only a minority of the commission's members had insisted on adding the phrase "and whose impending death is inevitable."

122. NVVE, "Fact Sheet," 3. The NVVE, moreover, notes that were it not for certain "confessional and dogmatic" factions within the CDA, euthanasia legislation would already have been enacted given what seems to be overwhelming public and parliamentary support. This interpretation, though from a partisan organization, seems entirely correct.

123. Feber, "Vicissitudes," 465.

124. Ibid.

125. Ibid.

126. Whether this empowerment would take the form of a legal instrument or simply a written request left with one's physician or family is unclear.

127. Although termination of treatment for unconscious patients and euthanasia for competent patients remain—at least formally—distinct issues, Sutorius and Admiraal both mentioned, independently, that the fear of an indeterminate and immobile existence does play a part in the overwhelming public support for euthanasia legislation.

128. Feber, "Vicissitudes," 466.

129. Roose, personal interview.

130. Dupuis, personal interview. Dr. Dupuis, in fact, likens the current situation to a "sort of experiment, with many variations." Out of this variation, she feels, will come a standard of practice that will have more general acceptance than if a law had been passed earlier.

131. Sutorius, personal interview.

132. In the parliamentary election of May 1986, the Christian Democratic Party (CDA), though it increased its representation in the lower house, was still forced to enter into coalition with the more conservative VVD party. Enough elements in *both* parties were opposed to euthanasia legislation to threaten the coalition. After the Council of State ruled in July of that same year that although euthanasia "might be admissible in some circumstance" it still recommended against changing the laws, opposition to euthanasia in both parties hardened. (NVVE, "Fact Sheet," 3).

133. "Speaking unofficially, the government is still trying to find out how far it can be involved. But now that euthanasia has such wide acceptance, this becomes a political question, it is a matter of words and definitions that will make everyone happy" (Rigter, personal interview).

134. Ibid.

135. Some have objected to my posing the question this way. If euthanasia is a matter of a right to self-determination about the time and methods of one's own death, setting an arbitrary limit on its frequency already restricts this principle of self-determination (Margaret Battin, personal communication). Without discounting the logic of the objection, it seems obvious that the Dutch themselves place limits on self-determination in this matter. If the practice were well-reported and reached such a level that it were considered routine, the Dutch, one senses, would act in some way to restrict euthanasia.

136. An excellent, concise, and current summary of the Dutch health care system is found in Nationale Ziekenhuisraad (National Hospital Association), *Health Care in the Netherlands* (Utrecht: Nationale Ziekenhuisraad, 1987). For a more comprehensive (but less current) analysis, see Harmen A. Tiddens, Joep P. Heesters, and Joost M. van de Zande, "Health Services in the Netherlands," in Marshall W. Raffels, ed., *Comparative Health Care Systems* (University Park, Pa.: 1984).

137. One health official, Herman H. van der Kloot Meijburg, who works in policy development for the Nationale Ziekenhuisraad (National Hospital Association), points to the obvious: "Even a survey would be like asking doctors, 'We know this is illegal, but do you do it?' It is too delicate for this present government to be asking such questions. Perhaps if they changed their official stand [that euthanasia should not be decriminalized], then they could ask more freely" (personal interview, Utrecht, 26 January 1989).

138. Whether or not they have researched this question more privately is a different matter. Before I traveled to the Netherlands, two sources had suggested to me that unofficially the KNMG had been monitoring the practice for several years. The representative of the KNMG with whom I spoke upon my arrival, however, denied that any such records were kept.

139. For reasons I discuss in the following section and in Chapter 4, notifying a prosecutor, especially one with whom the physician has established an understanding, involves less bureaucratic entanglement than writing "euthanasia" as a cause of death.

140. For example, the Dutch boast four well-staffed centers for the study of bioethics (in Amsterdam, Leiden, Utrecht, and Maastricht), and this in a country with one-twentieth the population of the United States.

141. Nevertheless, Dr. Dupuis declined to give a figure (or even a range) on the prevalence of the practice: "No one knows, and that is why we need a law, not another study, a law to control the practice" (personal interview).

142. Personal interview.

143. Meijburg, personal interview.

144. Rigter, Borst-Eilers, and Leenen, "Euthanasia," 1593. The article says "2% of all deaths that occur in family practice," but it does not mention that 70% of deaths in the Netherlands occur in institutions.

145. Reported in A. P. Olieman and H. J. G. Nijhius, "Euthansie in de huisartspraktijk" (Euthanasia in family practice), *Medisch Contact* 41 (1986): 691. Note that the study surveyed *only* family practitioners and that the range was extrapolated from a sample of only twenty-five general practitioners in the Hague.

146. Personal interview.

147. Amsterdam Department of Public Health, *General Report* (Amsterdam, 1987). Dr. Admiraal had a copy, which he showed me, but I was unable to obtain one for myself from the department.

148. Personal interview. Mr. Rigter suggests that the Amsterdam study probably underestimated the prevalence, based on private sources of information (which he declined to reveal).

149. C. I. Dessaur and C. J. C. Rutenfrans, *Mag de dokter doden?* (May the doctor kill?) (Amsterdam: Querido Editions, 1986).

150. Sutorius, who still has many contacts in the ministry from his days as a prosecutor, says that the exact number for 1987 was 197 (personal interview).

151. British Medical Association, *Euthanasia* (London: British Medical Association, 1988).

152. Rigter, Borst-Eilers, and Leenen, "Euthanasia," 1593.

153. Oliemans and Nijhuis, "Euthanasia," 691.

154. Tiddens, Heesters, and Van de Zande, "Health Service," 732.

155. This latter figure is cited in Nationale Ziekenhuisraad, "Health Care," 3.

156. Admiraal, personal interview.

157. Personal interview.

158. Ibid.

159. Personal interview.

160. Dr. Els Borst-Eilers, vice president of the Netherlands Health Council (personal interview, the Hague, 16 January 1989). She went on to add that claims that euthanasia is a recent phenomenon in the Netherlands were untrue: "This is not a 'new morality' that some say it is. We talked with many older doctors who said that they had done such a thing for many years. Perhaps what is new is more honest doctors, and now, perhaps, we will know better what is actually the case with euthanasia." She further agreed with Rigter's estimate of from five thousand to ten thousand cases per year, though she added that she thought it was probably much closer to the lower figure.

161. Ibid.

162. Dessaur and Ruttenfrans, *May the Doctor Kill?*, 399–407.

163. Ibid.

164. Dr. Richard Fenigsen, personal interview, s' Hertogenbosch, 18 January 1989.

165. Recently, for example, a well-publicized article written by a prestigious panel of

physicians in the United States cited a private source that suggested that euthanasia is practiced between five thousand and ten thousand times per year; see Sidney H. Wanzer, Daniel D. Federman, S. J. Adelstein, et al., "The Physician's Responsibility Toward Hopelessly Ill Patients: A Second Look" *New England Journal of Medicine* 320 (31 March 1989): 844–49.
166. Based on 120,000 deaths per year in the Netherlands (Nationale Ziekenhuisraad, "Health Care," 3).
167. A. Th. L. van Thiel, "Euthanasia in Holland," *News Exchange* 97 (n.d.), a publication of the World Federation of Doctors Who Respect Human Life (Ostend, Belgium).
168. Two possible exceptions to this sweeping generalization, however, may be found in H. W. A. Hilhorst, *Euthanasie in het ziekenhuis* (Euthanasia in the hospital) (De Tijdstroom: Lochem-Poperinge, 1983) and E. G. H. Kenter, "Euthanasie in een huisartspraktijk" (Euthanasia in family medicine), *Medisch Contact* 38 (23 September 1983): 1179–83. Both studies have their detractors—on opposite sides of the question. I return to this question of empirical evidence in the following chapter.

3 Describing the Practice of Euthanasia: Questions, Methods, and Case Studies

1. Statement of the VNMG to the Hague Court of Appeals, 1981 (cited in Feber, "Vicissitudes," 460).
2. See, for example, Dr. Helene Dupuis's comments above (Chapter 2, note 11). It is not that the frequency of euthanasia is altogether unimportant to them but that it is less important if one considers assistance with suicide a basic component of human self-determination.
3. Thus, Admiraal became irritated at my persistent questioning on the prevalence of euthanasia:

> Ask a different question: If people have a right to this, because it is humane, because it is better than dying alone, in pain, like some animal, how to do it correctly? How to make sure that people do not become forced [to accede] to it, how to make sure that doctors are doing this correctly. The other—even if it happens only few times—is an act of murder. (Personal interview.)

I would come back to this latter problem later in my discussions with Admiraal; see Chapter 4.
4. See, for example, Herman H. van der Kloot Meijburg, "De pijnlijke dood van Mevrouw V." (The painful death of Mrs. V.), *Medisch Contact* 42 (13 February 1987): 205–7.
5. I note two possible exceptions here. E. G. H. Kenter, a family doctor, gives clinical cases of seven patients euthanasized in "Euthanasie in een huisartspraktijk" (Euthanasia in one family practice), *Medisch Contact* 38 (23 September 1983): 1179–83; and H. W. A. Hilhorst, a medical sociologist, traces termination of treatment decisions in six hospitals in *Euthanasie in het ziekenhuis* (Euthanasia in the hospital) (De Tijdstroom: Lochem-Poperinge, 1983). Both

studies have been criticized: Kenter's, because he uses more unorthodox methods of euthanasia (potassium chloride injections, for example) and because he does not make clear how (or with whom) he determined that euthanasia was appropriate; and Hilhorst's, because he mixes termination-of-treatment decisions with active euthanasia in his cases, and thus the phenomenon he is describing is unclear.

6. I specifically left the wording vague initially so as not to be rebuffed out of hand.

7. And whether, for example, I was in some way involved with an investigation. Their guardedness was understandable.

8. Their responses varied. Some declined because of lack of time or interest in my project, others suggested dates too far into the future, and one wanted to know how I had gotten her phone number and why I was involved in such a project. I had been warned by several people that the Dutch resented the way they were being characterized on this issue abroad and that many would simply be unwilling to speak with a foreigner.

9. The first interviewer, for example, said that notes were one thing but an actual recording quite another ("I can say that you did not hear me correctly, or that your notes do not represent the truth . . . but a recording has my own voice on it.")

10. Respectively, Henk Rigter (Health Council of the Netherlands), Dr. Helene Dupuis (University of Leiden), and Pieter Admiraal (Reiner de Graaf Hospital in Delft).

11. Rigter and Dupuis were less sure of whether guideline 10, the documentation of the act of euthanasia, was necessarily a "guideline" as it was understood in the Netherlands. That it remained, technically, a point of law was agreed. Admiraal, on the other hand, considered it an important point to include, which I did.

12. Admiraal, for example, with whom I tried to pretest the guidelines sheet and the structured questionnaire, asked, half-jokingly, if this was "an inquisition or an interview to learn something new." Another physician, who became irritated when I asked "incredible questions that make me forget the story," suggested that I let him relate the clinical cases first, then ask questions to clarify points that seemed vague, "but do not ask so many questions that no one can answer."

13. Adapted from Takken, "Mercy-killing," 4. Takken's English version of the guidelines seems the most up-to-date; she cites as her source the report of the Health Council on euthanasia, "Advies inzake Euthanasie" (Advice on Euthanasia), which has the advantage of having been delivered long after the earlier court decisions, and on advice of both the KNMG and individual practitioners that gave testimony on the subject.

14. I was unprepared, for example, for the antipathy toward foreigners that had arisen in the past year over reports on the practice of euthanasia published abroad. One health official, before answering my questions, asked if I was going to write another "terrible story about those 'bad Dutch' who kill their weaklings?" Another suggested that if I was looking for an example of injustice in medical practice, I could easily have stayed in the United States and have had "enough information for several dissertations, I should think." I also underestimated how much national pride was at stake here. The Dutch do discuss eutha-

nasia freely and openly in their own press, but they are much more guarded in what they publish abroad. Articles by the Dutch that have appeared in English-language journals, for example, have been less an attempt to describe the practice than to justify its existence. The publication of a summary of the British Medical Association's statement on euthanasia (which was highly critical of the Dutch and came out just weeks before my arrival in the Netherlands) stung officials in the Netherlands and made me the (unintended) focus of a great deal of anger.

15. For example, I had originally intended to ask the physicians about the first two cases of euthanasia they had performed and the last two (hoping to capture possible changes in their practice and to avoid, to some extent, self-selection of the least controversial cases). This request was unworkable. Either people said they could not remember their first cases in detail, or they insisted on relating cases with which they felt most comfortable.

16. For example, when a physician gave only one underlying pathology for a patient that he or she had euthanized, I would invariably ask if there were other signs or symptoms pointing to diseases that—though not necessarily lethal—contributed to the overall state of the patient's health.

17. One doctor, for example, noted that there had been "much family discussion" on a particular patient's request for euthanasia, then said the family was in complete accord with the request for euthanasia. Initially, his phrase had suggested to me that there was some dissent within the family circle; on follow-up, he said that what he had meant was that the situation had been thoroughly aired by the family.

18. Source B, for example, a general practitioner, never consulted a third-party before performing euthanasia. Each time this source finished a narrative, I would come back to this point, to Source B's immense displeasure. By the end of the third narrative, Source B said, "And no, I did not get a second opinion . . . because I know my patients better than you or some other doctor . . . and that is all I have to say anymore." The interview, which had been gladly granted, took place at the source's office after hours, and I was told the source had "as much time as you need for an important subject as this." The interview, which began on so friendly and expansive a note, ended abruptly after forty-five minutes.

19. For example, one could suggest that those who agreed to speak were more acclimated to the practice than others who, though having practiced euthanasia, found it painful, embarrassing, or too personal a subject to be discussed with a stranger. Whether or not this presumed difference would alter the actual *practice* of euthanasia is also a matter of conjecture, but the possibility needs to be considered.

20. Rigter, Borst-Eilers, and Leenen, for example, in their article "Euthanasia Across the North Sea," 1593.

21. Admiraal, personal interview.

22. I should mention here again that all interviews were conducted in English; words that had no easy translation (such as *ontluisteren*) were transcribed, then translated by an interpreter. Where the syntax became too tortured, the appropriate English phrase (in brackets) was inserted. Unless noted otherwise, the interviewees' command of English was generally adequate and in most cases excellent.

23. Some, for example, said that earlier cases (going back to the early 1980s) were blurred in their memories; others simply avoided the question altogether.
24. For example, where I was more likely to emphasize the clinical condition of the patient—and the effect it might have on a patient's ability to choose euthanasia freely—the interpreter would emphasize the physician's insistence that the patient had requested euthanasia, and the documentation of that fact.

4 From Public Theory to Private Practice: Evaluation of Case Studies

1. William Roose, foreign secretary of the NVVE, personal interview, Amsterdam, 26 January 1989.
2. This, at least, is how I interpret the KNMG's collaborative statement on euthanasia with the nurses' association, which suggested that if questioned, a doctor or a nurse could appeal to the principle of confidentiality in legal proceedings (KNMG, "Guidelines," 437).
3. F. L. Meijler, "Geneeskunde en Euthanasie" (Medicine and Euthanasia), *Nederlands Tijdschrift voor Geneeskunde* 130 (1986), cited in Takken, "Mercy-killing," 4–5.
4. Avedis Donabedian's influential evaluation techniques, which judge medical practices by the outcomes they produce for patients, assume that there are established structures and well-defined processes influencing those outcomes. More importantly, the model he uses also assumes general agreement on what a desirable outcome is for a patient; in Donabedian, "Evaluating the Quality of Medical Care," *Milbank Memorial Fund Quarterly* 44 (1966): 166–206. See also P. M. Ellwood, "Outcomes Management: A Technology of Patient Experience," *New England Journal of Medicine* 318 (9 January 1988): 1549–56; A. Laupacis, D. L. Sackett, and R. S. Roberts, "An Assessment of Clinically Useful Measures of the Consequences of Treatment," *New England Journal of Medicine* 318 (30 June 1988): 1728–34.
5. Definitions of what precisely the prudent exercise of free will entails will vary wildly, depending on how heavy an emphasis one gives to the principle of patient autonomy. Nevertheless, everyone with whom I spoke seemed agreed that patients needed to receive and understand as much information about their situation as was possible. One physician (in source I), for example, saw the function performed on the terminal-care team precisely in these terms, as an educator: "My job is for the patient to understand everything else we can do to help without euthanasia."
6. Even the notion of a terminal illness proved too vague for the Leeuwarden court to accept as a necessary condition; the inability of the medical profession to predict, with accuracy and regularity, what a "terminal case" was made it an unsuitable substitute for a person's private choice (Feber, "Vicissitudes," 440). If one has to deal in ambiguities, better that the ambiguity derive from the personal judgment of a patient (who, after all, would bear the consequences of his or her choice) than from an outside party less affected by the decision.
7. The legal standing of such declarations in these sorts of cases in the Netherlands

is still unclear to me. The NVVE has made available to its members "euthanasia tags" (similar to the emergency medical treatment tags worn, for example, by diabetics), which declare the person's preference for euthanasia over certain existences. I do not know whether or how often physicians act on the basis of such declarations. Eugene Sutorius notes, however, that Living Will declarations, though not as prevalent as in the United States, are made in the Netherlands and that some include stipulations under which euthanasia may be performed (personal interview).

8. The University of Utrecht Hospital, for example, has written up a protocol specifying that a request for euthanasia may be considered legitimate only if it can be documented that the patient made such a request absent the presence of family or friends ("Guidelines for Assistance in Suicide and Voluntary Active Euthanasia in Cases of Incurable, Physically Sick Patients," Utrecht, 1985). To avoid any misunderstanding here, I should note that none of the cases collected in this study come from the University of Utrecht Hospital.

9. One institution, in which some of the collected cases of euthanasia occurred (and which therefore is not named), notes that the family "is an important consideration" in these matters. The physician elaborating on this policy, however, saw this as a check against poorly considered requests for euthanasia: "Sometimes . . . we see a family that talks out a patient from euthanasia . . . the patient sees that the family still loves them, and that suicide is not a good plan for them."

10. One should point out here that the Dutch have yet to develop either legal or professional guidelines on termination of treatment for patients incapable of giving consent. The Dutch have chosen to address the issue of voluntary euthanasia first, in part because they give such great weight to the principle of patient autonomy. To the Dutch, the issue of termination or withdrawal of treatment from incompetent or decisionally incapable patients is a potentially more fractious problem. I return to this particular issue in Chapter 5.

11. The issue of euthanasia in children receives scant treatment in this study because the guidelines do not address themselves directly to this problem. Moreover, I only encountered one case involving a child. Some (the KNMG, for example) have suggested that for minors (which, in the Netherlands, means children under sixteen years of age), it would be preferable to have the parents in agreement before euthanasia is performed, but they decline to give the parents veto power over a child's decision to request euthanasia.

12. The physician disputed this interpretation during our interview: "It was obvious . . . to everyone what was wanted here." Nevertheless, the physician could not point to specific documentation in which the parents expressly called for euthanasia.

13. Margaret Battin, with whom I have had a friendly disagreement on this issue, claims that I make too much of the influence of professional judgment in these matters (personal communication, Chicago, 20 May 1989).

14. William Roose adds a similar comment: "Doctors here are not like Belgian doctors, with all the pomposity, and certainly not like German or American doctors. Here, doctors are just chaps, like any other of us. They just do a job. And all the talk you have about 'professional ethics' is a way of disguising what you

really think: that you know what is good for the patient better than the patient does. Well, here in the Netherlands we don't think that way" (personal interview).

15. Leenen, for example, insists on the following distinction:

> Problems such as abortion, euthanasia, etc. are not liable to medical ethics but to general ethical judgment. It is not the medical profession which has to set norms. One must distinguish between medical acts and social acts in which doctors are involved. Medical acts can in principle be judged on the basis of professional norms by the profession itself; for the judgment on the permissibility of euthanasia no medical professional norms exist. ("Euthanasia," 201.)

But Leenen later notes, approvingly, that even this "social act" is restricted to assistance rendered only by a physician.

16. Admiraal, "Active Voluntary Euthanasia" (reprint of a speech given by Dr. Admiraal in London to the Voluntary Euthanasia Society, 14 April 1985).

17. Personal interview.

18. See, for example, T. J. Starr et al., "Quality of Life and Resuscitation Decisions in Elderly Patients," *Journal of General Internal Medicine* 1 (November/December, 1986): 373–79; and, R. A. Pearlman and R. F. Uhlmann, "Quality of Life in Chronic Diseases: Perceptions of Elderly Patients," *Journal of Gerontology* 43 (1988): M25–30.

19. One should note, however, that at the request of the NVVE, Admiraal authored the first book published by a physician in the Netherlands that outlined not only the guidelines under which euthanasia was permitted but also listed recommended drugs and dosages to accomplish the task (P. V. Admiraal, "Justifiable Euthanasia: A Manual for the Medical Profession" [Amsterdam: NVVE, 1980]).

20. Personal interview.

21. If the reader views this story with some skepticism, I admit that I was suspicious too when Dr. van der Meer first related it. I asked him to repeat the story, which he did without changing the details, adding only that this was not his patient but that he had been called to the case (as a member of the hospital ethics committee) after the euthanasia attempt failed.

22. "Look," he says by way of an example, "at other things done in medicine not very frequently—at replacing parts [organs]. We do this, too, but not many times; but we must have ways of testing such a thing" (personal interview).

23. Personal interview.

24. Admiraal, "Voluntary Euthanasia," 4.

25. On this particular point, Admiraal suggests that the guidelines may give too much latitude. He notes, for example, that he fulfills the letter of the stipulation by consulting with another medical colleague but that the colleague is one whom he knows is "friendly" and from whom concurrence on the matter is almost *pro forma* (personal interview).

26. Rigter, Borst-Eilers, and Leenen, "Euthanasia."

27. Personal interview.

28. Personal interview. Sutorius notes, moreover, that because of Admiraal's notoriety in this field, "he is closely watched; he has to be careful" (personal interview).

29. Personal interview.
30. Ibid.
31. Personal interview.
32. I. van der Sluis, "How Voluntary Is Voluntary Euthanasia?" *Journal of Palliative Care* 4 (1988): 107–9.
33. J. H. Segers, "Elderly Persons on the Subject of Euthanasia," *Issues in Law and Medicine* 4 (1988): 407–26.
34. Nieuw Vrijthof, "Beleidnotitie (actieve) euthanasie" (Notice on [active] euthanasia) (Tiel: Nieuw Vrijthof, 1986).
35. Personal interview, anonymity requested.
36. Personal interview, anonymity requested.
37. Personal interview, anonymity requested.
38. This case was originally brought to my attention by Dr. Fenigsen because, as he said, "others will not talk to you about this." However, the details of the case were confirmed by Admiraal, and again by Sutorius, who—because he was involved in the case—could not speak freely, but when I read the story back to him as I had heard it, he told me that it was "not incorrect."
39. "The KNMG said that this was a young doctor and that he could be disciplined in other ways" (Admiraal, personal interview).
40. "But," says Admiraal, "this is like kicking him out; he would never be able to practice again after such a public rebuke."
41. Mr. Rigter and Dr. Borst-Eilers, at the Health Council of the Netherlands, for example, said that this case was a "disaster" from the very beginning and that it would be misleading to draw any conclusions from it (personal interview).
42. Even Mr. Sutorius, who earlier expressed his reservations about the current state of judicial oversight, agrees on this point: "What we should have is a sort of count [accounting], so that doctors have to defend what they have already done. But to do so before that act? I cannot tell you what it means to suffer for you; when it happens to me, I will know. But I cannot say before what happens what it will be" (personal interview). The law, or a more tightly descriptive regulatory scheme, is thus useless.
43. The nature of the disease, its extent and natural history, laboratory values, physical signs—all these criteria, while not decisive, would at least allow one to evaluate the reasonableness, for example, of a determination of a terminal illness.
44. Recall, for example, Dr. Admiraal's refusing euthanasia to the young woman who was dying from leukemia and whose parents refused to let her lover move in; similarly, there are Dr. van der Meer's two stories of refusing euthanasia because he saw alternative solutions.
45. By suggesting the absence of alternative solutions, for example, or as in the case of Admiraal, by laying out the possibility of euthanasia to a patient before the patient has asked.

5 The Dangers of Regulating an Active Death: Summary and Conclusions

1. Erasmus, quoted in Margaret Mann Phillips, *The "Adages" of Erasmus* (Cambridge: Cambridge University Press, 1964), 211. Erasmus's comment on the

Dutch appears in Simon Schama's remarkable book on Dutch manners and morals in the Renaissance, *The Embarrassment of Riches: An Interpretation of Dutch Culture in the Golden Age* (London: Fontana Press, 1987), 7.

2. H. Tristram Engelhardt, "Suicide and the Cancer Patient," *CA—A Cancer Journal for Clinicians* 36 (March/April 1986): 105.

3. On this very issue of euthanasia, Engelhardt points approvingly to the paradigm of the Netherlands; see his "Death by Free Choice: Variations on an Antique Theme," in *Suicide and Euthanasia,* ed. Baruch Brody (Dordrecht: Kluwer Academic Publishers, 1989), 251–80.

4. D. Brahams, "Euthanasia in the Netherlands," *Lancet* 335 (1990): 591.

5. Pieter Admiraal, for example, made a great point of noting that he keeps "very good records, so that no one can later say, 'This was murder, not euthanasia.' I always tell doctors who are going to practice euthanasia that the documents are very important, because no notes will mean trouble for them" (personal interview).

6. Dr. van der Meer, for example, said that long before the guidelines were issued, he made it a point to get a "friendly doctor" to cosign the patient's chart, so that there would later be no doubt as to what had transpired. For the same reasons, Dr. Admiraal has a small group of colleagues who act as cosignatories on his progress notes.

7. Rigter, Borst-Eilers, and Leenen, "Euthanasia," 1593.

8. H. J. J. Leenen, "Euthanasia in the Netherlands," in *Medicine, Medical Ethics, and the Value of Life,* ed. Peter Byrne (New York: John Wiley & Sons, 1990), 13.

9. Dr. Helene Dupuis, for example, suggested as much in her interview. There is now enough information, she said, to get an idea of how euthanasia would be realized and what problems would need to be addressed to control the practice.

10. Eugene Sutorius, for one, suggests that the commission made a major mistake in this matter, for it might have been able to make a stronger case to the queen had it spoken with more unanimity. More importantly, though, Sutorius also points out that the commission's deliberations accurately reflect the difficulty in restricting a right to euthanasia once it has been determined that autonomy is an overriding principle (personal interview).

11. British Medical Association, *Euthanasia: Report of the Working Party to Review the British Medical Association's Guidance on Euthanasia* (London: British Medical Association, 1988). For a strong critique of the BMA report, see Peter Byrne, "The BMA on Euthanasia: The Philosopher Versus the Doctor," in *Medicine, Medical Ethics, and the Value of Life,* ed. Peter Byrne (New York: John Wiley & Sons, 1990), 15–33. A similarly negative view of the BMA report is also found in Institute of Medical Ethics Working Party of the Ethics of Prolonging Life and Assisting Death, "Assisted Death," *Lancet* 336 (1990): 610–13. In this sense, the British situation is analogous to the current American position: the professional medical associations in both countries are publicly against euthanasia, yet there is a strong and persistent dissent against this prohibition both within and outside the ranks of the medical profession.

12. In fact, in its current formulation, Dutch policy allows *only* physicians to engage in this practice.

13. Engelhardt, "Death by Free Choice," 264–65.

14. See, for example, Kass, "Neither for Love nor Money"; Kamisar, "Some Non-Religious Views"; and, most recently, William Reichel and Arthur J. Dyck, "Euthanasia: A Contemporary Moral Quandary," *Lancet* 334 (1989): 1321–23.
15. Kass, "Is There a Medical Ethic?"
16. On this very point—the obligations engendered by other persons' vulnerabilities—there is a remarkably powerful and well-sustained argument in Robert E. Goodin, *Protecting the Vulnerable: A Reanalysis of Our Social Responsibilities* (Chicago: University of Chicago Press, 1985). Although Goodin's analysis draws little from medical matters, his study has important implications for the conduct, and the obligations, of physicians towards their patients.
17. Charles L. Sprung makes a controversial argument to this effect in "Changing Attitudes and Practices in Forgoing Life-Sustaining Treatments," *Journal of the American Medical Association* 263 (1990): 2211–15. Sprung worries that the general trend over the past fifteen years in the United States in adjudicating "right-to-die" cases has paved the way legally and (perhaps more importantly) philosophically for active euthanasia in the United States.
18. Engelhardt goes further, moreover, and sees the Dutch as "a light to the world" in this matter (in "Death by Free Choice," p. 265).
19. Christine K. Cassel and Diane E. Meier, "Morals and Moralism in the Debate over Euthanasia and Assisted Suicide," *New England Journal of Medicine* 323 (1990): 751.
20. William F. May, "Ethical Considerations in Life and Death Decisions," in *Life and Death Issues,* eds. James E. Hamner and Barbara J. Sax Jacobs (Memphis: University of Tennessee Press), 63–64.
21. Brahams, "Euthanasia," 591.
22. H. J. J. Leenen, "Coma Patients in the Netherlands," *British Medical Journal* 300 (1990): 69.
23. For a well-argued essay to this effect, see Robert F. Weir and Larry Gostin, "Decisions to Abate Life-Sustaining Treatment for Nonautonomous Patients: Ethical Standards and Legal Liability for Physicians After *Cruzan,*" *Journal of the American Medical Association* 264 (1990): 1846–53.
24. David Orentlicher, "Physician Participation in Assisted Suicide," *Journal of the American Medical Association* 262 (1989): 1844–45.
25. Sidney H. Wanzer, Daniel D. Federman, S. J. Adelstein, et al., "The Physician's Responsibility Toward Hopelessly Ill Patients: A Second Look," *New England Journal of Medicine* 320 (30 March 1989): 844–49.

Index